How To Market Your Plugin

A Framework for the Sleep-Deprived Developer

By Bridget Willard

Foreword by Adrian Tobey

Published by BridgetWillard.com

ISBN: 9798702512228

Printed in the United States of America

Dedication

This book is dedicated to my dear friend, Rhonda Negard, who has encouraged me to share more of my technical knowledge over the past five months. I'm so lucky to have a friend like you in my life. Truly. (I'd put #Blessed here if it didn't annoy me so much. LOLZ)

Acknowledgements

Sarah Pressler! You're the best. I needed a tough editor -- and a great friend -- like you.

Thanks for designing my book art, Rhonda Negard, a nod to 007 -- my fav. I love it so much.

"Hey yo" and many thanks to Devin Walker for allowing me to use the GiveWP trademark as well as to you and Jason Knill for allowing me to help you build the GiveWP brand back in the day.

Thanks to Jason Tucker who invited me to co-host Smart Marketing Show on the WPwatercooler Network the last 5.5 years. (The podcast is formerly known as WPblab.)

Thanks to my clients who believed in me and allowed me to help your brand whether it was a long or short duration. I know it's not easy to trust a vendor with your assets.

Many thanks to the WordPress Community for welcoming me in, allowing me to speak at conferences, and to Andrea Middleton for recruiting me to join the Make WordPress Marketing Team.

Table of Contents

Foreword

A Marketing Case Study

By Adrian Tobey
CEO and Founder of Groundhogg.io

Background

Groundhogg had 2 problems.

Problem #1

We were bootstrapping it. We didn't have money to buy ads or pay for marketing services.

Problem #2

We had developed the first WordPress CRM utility tool of its kind so the real challenge is choosing the category to sell it in. Should we position it as a Marketing Automation tool or a CRM tool? Which was the better strategy to get faster market penetration?

With no budget to market, in a product category that had monster competitors like Active

Campaign, Infusionsoft, Hubspot, etc, we had a GOLIATH mountain to climb.

We scoured the internet to find help on "how to market a WordPress plugin." We did hundreds of Google Searches, YouTube Searches, Twitter searches to find any business intelligence that would give us golden nuggets on how to market our new WordPress plugin. Save for a couple of dated articles, there was nothing.

We launched anyway. We went in blind. We improvised. It took 2 years to get to 3,000+ active users and 25KMRR.

Here are five business intelligence golden nuggets we wish we would have known sooner that would have saved us time, money, and headaches.

1. Price your plugin correctly.

We used the Freemium model. We offered huge value at a low price -- and it cost us sales. Gratefully, more seasoned WordPress developers helped us see the light. We had a pricing problem. Once we corrected our pricing, we became a profitable business. If you're too cheap, no one will believe it's a good product. Unless you have a big existing tribe to give a deal to, create hype, get your affiliates to sell it, create buzz and get mass adoption, I recommend you avoid being the cheapest on the market, or too low in price.

2. Did you know that you can SEO your listing on WordPress Repo?

Optimize your listing. This was HUGE for us in terms of ranking & attracting new prospects. Pay attention to details in your listing and optimize it!

3. Make friends!

We would have NEVER survived without the mentorship of other WordPress Plugin Developers. There are groups you can join, masterminds, events, etc. We can't overstate how important this was in our development. We have eternal gratitude to fellow developers who have been instrumental in our growth and success. The best investment you could make is right here. When you choose an integration, make friends with the developers. Most will help market you to their tribes and help them in return.

4. Obsess about giving great service.

If you read our reviews in the WordPress repo, 9 out of 10 reviews will be about our "service." It took us a long while to understand this was the MOST important thing to our users. It wasn't "how great our product was," but about "how great our service is." If I could share something personal with you, build this muscle first. Your product could be amazing, but if you lack the will of giving good "service," you'll struggle. WordPress users expect high value and excellent service. Obsess about it. Become great at it. This affects "word of mouth" sales. Again, critical in the WordPress universe.

5. Be Transparent in your story.

Know your story! Then spend a significant amount of time reaching out to podcasters, WordPress writers, other developers, etc who will listen to your story. Be 100% authentic (don't hype). Tell them exactly what you have, the problem it solves, where you're at, you need help, etc. Transparency is key. We got interviews when we only had 50 users. We landed HUGE interviews with just 2000 users. We were telling our story -- with full transparency -- and found people would rally around us regardless of how small we were. We had zero clout, yet these people rallied around us to help us acquire new customers. They held us up while we got to 3,000 users at 25KMRR in 2 years. Not bad when we started with 0 prospects, 0 customers, 0 marketing budget, and 0 reviews! It can be done!

BONUS NUGGET: Launch!

There is nowhere to get it unless you launch. Yes, you'll make mistakes. People will forgive you for them. Your users will tell you what problems to solve next. They will help you and guide you. All you have to do is give them a platform to share their thoughts (i.e. Facebook group), and then listen. When I started Groundhogg, I was a business of 1. 100% programmer. Over the last 2 years, I've become 80% listener and 20% programmer. As you mature, your product matures. A team evolves. And the best lessons will always come from being a very good listener.

Find Out More

https://wordpress.org/plugins/groundhogg/#reviews

https://www.youtube.com/channel/UChHW8I3wPv-KUhQ
YX-eUp6g

groundhogg.io/

https://www.linkedin.com/in/adriantobey/

Groundhogg Twitter: @Groundhoggwp

Adrian's Twitter: @adriantobey

Introduction

Developers often ask me, "How do I sell my plugin?" or "How do I get more downloads?"

Well, this book is for you: the WordPress developer, the engineer, the person behind the code. Providing a culmination of the knowledge I've gained working as a professional content marketer for the last 12+ years, you hold a book that empowers you with the actionable steps needed to develop, deploy, and maintain an effective marketing plan.

Gaining a strategic overview of the ideal marketing campaigns and scenarios will help you make the best decisions for your marketing budget. And budget issues are genuine – both in terms of time and money. You may not have quite the funding to "market all the things." But that is 100% okay because the best way to market anything is in phases. Just like how you develop in sprints, marketing is best handled with the same strategy and execution.

So, whether you outsource a marketer or do it yourself, reading the following chapters will put you in a better position to spend your marketing time and budget most effectively.

Chapter 1

How is Marketing Similar To Building?

It's easy to be overwhelmed and intimidated by marketing. It can easily feel like you're tooting your own horn or being like a used car salesman. No one wants to give off that vibe, even a used car salesman.

What's Marketing?

The American Marketing Association (AMA) defines marketing as:

"Marketing is the activity, set of institutions, and processes for creating, communicating, delivering, and exchanging offerings that have value for customers, clients, partners, and society at large. (Approved 2017)" (American Marketing Association)

In its essence, marketing is communication. Communication is based upon language. Language has structure, logic, and is a framework for larger works; it has the power to change society. Coding is also built upon language. It has structure, logic, and is a framework for larger works. Coding also has the power to change society for good.

So, how is marketing like coding?

Marketing is like coding because it establishes a process for how to use language to achieve your goals -- to bring "value for customers, clients, partners, and society at large."(American Marketing Association)

As an engineer who understands many languages, you can also learn the framework of marketing. You know programming languages. You deeply understand problem-solving and possess the skills to engineer those solutions. You've spent thousands of hours honing your skills, learning frameworks, and developing your craft.

WordPress developers are engineers. As an engineer, you feel satisfaction from identifying and solving a complicated technical problem. It means you can think about issues, understand them, and see the paths to a solution.

> *"Building things allows us to think about them. Thinking about things allows us to*

understand them. It can save us money, give us a sense of gratification and value, and it can also give us another perspective on what others do." Warren Laine-Naida (Laine-Naida)

Marketing is a skill you are capable of learning. It is the deep understanding of the people your product helps. That understanding develops an empathy that is a path toward building relationships with potential customers, so they want to buy your product.

Programming is about human behavior. Marketing is about human behavior. Fortunately for us, both are relatively predictable.

Chapter 2

Why Would I Outsource Marketing?

There is a vast difference between whether you can learn something or whether it is the best use of your time. This is where delegation comes in. What can you outsource so your time can be best spent on high-level activities?

As an entrepreneur, it's hard to delegate. We're so attached to our ideas, our creation, and our workflows. This is a potential obstacle for us all. Almost every business consultant asks us to take a look at what we can hand off.

Sure, at first, you can probably handle your own marketing efforts. As your plugin scales, however, delegation is the key to growth. How so? Taking marketing off of your plate frees you to work on your product. This includes features, extensions, or subscription plans. These product improvements will keep your plugin front-and-center to your growing user base. The faster you can develop and deploy, the faster you can increase your number of active installs, customers, and recurring revenue.

Should I Find a Partner?

Partnering with an experienced business partner will ease the burden of the product launch. If you prefer to hire a marketer, that person can work with you and your staff by taking tasks outlined in this book off of your hands. Product managers and support staff help you focus on what you do best during, through, and during product iteration.

You can do any combination of the three: bring in a partner, hire an employee, or contract a vendor. It all depends upon your business model and your comfort level of delegating tasks.

1. You can bring a marketer in as a business partner. I've seen this work with several of my clients and well known WordPress plugin shops.

2. You can hire an employee who is the Marketing Manager.

3. You can contract with a marketing professional as a vendor; this is an easy way to get going until you can bring someone on staff.

Whether you decide to find a business partner, hire an employee to do marketing tasks, or outsource to a vendor or agency, this book gives you a framework for what currently works in the WordPress plugin ecosystem. The more informed you are, the better you can communicate with that person or persons.

How Do You Find a Marketing Professional?

You're at the point where it's time to delegate marketing. How do you find a marketing professional? The first resource is your peers on Twitter. You'd be surprised at how many people are well-connected and can put you in the right direction.

If you prefer to work with an agency, look for one who has worked with software and digital sales. Another great place to find marketing professionals is your local WordPress Meetup. Most likely, WordCamp speaker lists have a marketer or three.

Don't let budget stop you from reaching out. The marketing professional may create a custom plan just for you. You won't know until you ask them. For example, I offer customized services that I don't actively promote online or on my website. And I know others in the marketing space do the same. Though my rates are published, I listen to the prospect's problems and offer a solution that balances the scope of work with the budget available.

You may just need a bit of 1-to-1 coaching and accountability to get your marketing program up and running. You might not even know this is all you really need until you reach out and talk to someone in the marketing world.

But, What if You Can't Afford to Hire a Marketing Professional?

If your budget doesn't allow for an outside marketer, it will be up to you to market your plugin. Managing your marketing activities requires an active strategy on your part. Pay close attention to your marketing efforts just as you do your support tickets or development tasks. Otherwise it will be too easy to neglect marketing for more pressing development tasks. (Rarely do engineers neglect development for marketing.)

Support requests, however, can get out of hand quickly and drain away from your joy. Therefore, it is critical to find a productive balance in your workweek that allows for a dedicated amount of time to be spent on marketing, development, and support. And you may even get to the point where you want to outsource support. But that's another chapter.

I highly recommend time blocking[1] as a means to productivity flow. Set aside a few hours each week, over the course of a few days, to spend on marketing. Installing that regimen will allow you to work deeply on marketing. That regime will bring an increase in revenue directly related to your intentional marketing efforts. Soon, you will be in a position to delegate marketing.

---

[1] https://youtu.be/2812mKA23Vs

Chapter 3

An Overall Marketing Brief

A marketing brief is a core document that keeps your brand focused on its marketing goals. As we iterate product development, it's easy to chase after the next shiny thing. Resist the temptation. Stay focused on your goals.

An overall marketing brief is the framework for your marketing. What is your goal for this plugin in three years? What is the strategy to achieve that goal? What tactics will you employ?

It's too long to include here, so in the back of the book, "Add-on 1" includes a three-year framework. "Add-on 2" includes a sample overall marketing brief for your reference.

You can create sub-briefs, breaking down your tactics into more detailed marketing campaign briefs. For example, your marketing brief may mention social media channels as part of your overall strategy. To make the documents more manageable, creating a social media marketing brief allows you to stay focused with your measurement and reporting.

Regardless of the duration of your marketing brief, it should be reasonably straightforward and contain measurable goals.

Chapter 4

One Website to Rule them All

I encourage all of my clients to have one website to sell products and services. The biggest argument against this that I encounter is "My plugins aren't related to one another."

In your eyes, you may not see the connection. That's okay. Are they all eCommerce plugins? Great. They can be on the same website.

When I released LaunchWithWords.com, my WordPress plugin, I bought the domain and pointed it to a landing page on BridgetWillard.com. As I talk about this plugin on social media or podcasts, I have a memorable domain name. Though people type that in, they are coming to my "one website to rule them all."

One interesting thing I have seen in the last month since launching this plugin is that people go from the plugin landing page, to the starter content pack, to my services.

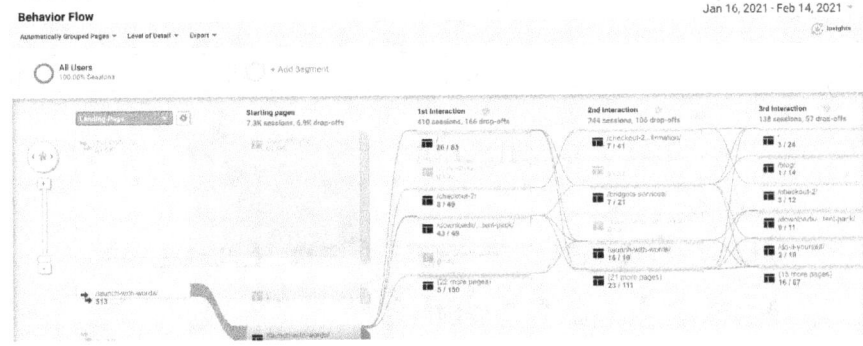

	Page	Pageviews ↓	Unique Pageviews	Avg. Time on Page	En
		8,760 % of Total: 100.00% (8,760)	**8,262** % of Total: 100.00% (8,262)	**00:01:57** Avg for View: 00:01:57 (0.00%)	
☐	1. /bot-traffic.icu	**5,040** (57.53%)	5,022 (60.78%)	00:00:00	
☐	2. /launch-with-words/	**643** (7.34%)	568 (6.87%)	00:02:45	
☐	3. /	**500** (5.71%)	416 (5.04%)	00:01:01	
☐	4. /downloads/launch-with-words-starter-content-pack/	**341** (3.89%)	280 (3.39%)	00:02:16	
☐	5. /bridgets-services/	**139** (1.59%)	120 (1.45%)	00:02:40	
☐	6. /blog/	**106** (1.21%)	64 (0.77%)	00:00:53	
☐	7. /checkout-2/	**99** (1.13%)	85 (1.03%)	00:00:39	
☐	8. /twitter-marketing/	**94** (1.07%)	86 (1.04%)	00:03:14	
☐	9. /bridgetwillardbio/	**77** (0.88%)	66 (0.80%)	00:02:06	
☐	10. /do-it-yourself/	**69** (0.79%)	56 (0.68%)	00:01:38	

Beside my bot traffic, I'm extremely happy with the last thirty days' worth of traffic.

- 643 to the product landing page

- 500 to home

- 341 to the download page

- 139 to my pricing page

- 106 to my blog

- 99 to the checkout

Just Because You Can, Doesn't Mean You Should

Big brands don't create websites just because they can. For example, Amazon.com has millions of products that aren't related, and they have one website. Macys.com has one website. The Sears Catalog was one book.

Look, I get it. It's fun to build a website around your product. However, it's also more work to maintain two websites vs one. You probably have to create a subdomain for documentation; that's enough work. Allow your plugin to benefit from your career and reputation.

Using one website also saves you time. Now you can work on marketing your product instead of maintaining auxiliary websites and social channels. And, if you keep building products with a website for each, you'll end up having to hire a developer to maintain all of your sites.

"What if I decide to sell my plugin?"

Most WordPress developers build a product because there is a problem that keeps arising. Having a product as an additional stream of revenue is an excellent way to diversify your WordPress agency's skillset and cash-flow. You may very well want to sell your plugin; rather, its users.

However, if you are building your plugin to sell it in three to five years, you may want to have a second website and separate social media accounts.

Be intentional with this effort. When you build your budget for the plugin, include the cost of website development and maintenance, alongside focused marketing efforts for that product. Build your business plan, deploy it, and then maintain it until you're ready to sell the plugin, the website, and the associated social media sites.

As mentioned in the sample marketing brief, it's a good idea to reserve usernames for your WordPress plugin on various social platforms. Then simply direct visitors to those accounts to your main social media accounts and market the plugin(s) from the main business feeds. If you decide to sell off the plugin, it will be easy to hand over the dedicated accounts to the new plugin owner and simply stop marketing the plugin on your main business accounts.

Chapter 5

What Project Management Software Should I use?

"The best tool is the one you use."

Bridget Willard

If you like Asana, use it. Basecamp, use it. Clickup, use it. You could go as far as to use a Google Sheet, though it isn't as efficient and won't scale as well.

My brilliant idea used to be setting up a marketing branch in GitHub that followed your product's dependencies. That is great for the one-person plugin shop if your marketer knows how to manage branched development repositories. (Not a common skill set among marketers!)

The point of the project management tool is to collaborate and delegate in an efficient way that can scale as your product/team grows. So, it's important to note that your software version control environment isn't a project management software. Using a git repo for marketing tasks fails when you bring in a marketing partner, hire a marketer, or contract with a vendor. The likelihood of them knowing how to manage a git repo is slim to none. Most marketers can't just get in there and submit pull requests. And, honestly now, how many of you really want a marketer muddling up your git repo with marketing tasks?

Having a growth mindset means putting the tools into place to help you grow. Those tools include project management software, team members, and a process that can be replicated. It means creating a space where people can learn what processes are in your mind. This comes with documentation; not just of your plugin, but of your whole process around development, deployment, and support.

Documenting your process means that people can cross train within your organization. If you are a solo-shop, consider partnering with another developer in the same situation. Should you want a vacation or need time to deal with family emergencies, this documentation will help your business survive. Being prepared in this way allows your business to survive without you for a day (because you're sick) or a week (vacation) or you pass away.

A great place to document the process is a project management software. You can and should have documentation elsewhere (Google Drive, for example) but once you create your process, that can be implemented with each iteration of your plugin within a project management tool.

Additionally, the history of what you did previously will be recorded in your project management tool. This allows you to hire new members and onboard them quickly. This is the beauty of a growth-mindset paired with a great PM tool.

It's not critically important which project management tool you choose. Basecamp, Asana, Trello, Clickup: they're all basically the same. The most important thing is that you use it consistently.

Within each project, define the tasks, estimate the time, plan your workflow, complete your to-do's, and work this into your routine. So choose your tool and use it. Don't spend more than a few hours deciding which tool to use. You'll fall into analysis paralysis which is a form of procrastination.

Example of a Task:

To-Do: Write Landing Page Copy for New Extension [2 hours]

Author of To Do: [Person A]

Due: [date]

Assigned to: [Person B]

Notes:

Write copy in this google doc (link).

The next step, have [person A] review it, make any corrections/iterations

Done = Google doc approved by and turned in to Person A

Chapter 6

Did You Test Your Plugin?

You've built your plugin.

Your documentation is growing.

You're consulting with a marketer.

You've set up your infrastructure.

Things are getting exciting!

But have you thoroughly tested your plugin?

Testing your plugin with your team is important. That's your alpha phase. There are many resources for environments to set up. I will leave that up to you. Make WordPress has a short resource on plugin unit tests in their documentation[2]. But, at some point, it will have to be tested in real-world environments -- with beta testers.

"Beta Testing is performed by 'real users' of the software application in 'real environment' and it can be considered as a form of external User

---

[2] https://make.wordpress.org/cli/handbook/misc/plugin-unit-tests/

<u>Acceptance Testing</u>. It is the final test before shipping a product to the customers." (Guru99)

What Does Beta Testing Have to Do With Marketing?

It's emotionally difficult to know when your plugin is ready enough for beta testers. The tendency I see from my clients is to continuously tweak their product out of fear.

> *"We should just put it out and let the world decide." Derek Sivers (Sivers)*

I totally understand. You may not think your product is ready; no one wants their code criticized. However, in order to market your plugin, you need beta testers. To get beta testers, you need a minimum viable product. The beta testing phase is where you build your marketing pipeline. So figure out when it's done enough and move forward.

Allowing beta testers to support your idea with real-world feedback will turn into word-of-mouth marketing. When a user is excited about your product, they will tell others. This is the beginning of the buzz everyone wants to conjure up.

If you can't think of people to beta test your plugin right off the top of your head, look to your local WordPress Meetup. You may even belong to a private Facebook or Slack group. Those are great places, too.

Beta testers can also give you reviews that can be repurposed in your plugin marketing. Put these reviews on your product's landing page, sales page, and in blog posts. Once two or three trusted peers test for you, you'll want to put up a landing page for more beta signups.

Share the landing page with reviews on social media. As people give you feedback, you can decide what milestone to incorporate those ideas. Are they mission critical for launch or shall you save them for 2.0?

Chapter 7

Build a Landing Page for Beta Signups

So you're on board getting beta testers. Beta users are your best testers. They will break your product if they can. Good. Fix it. That's what every software developer does. Even WordPress' Core Updates have issues.

How Do You Get Beta Testers?

You have to ask. You have to recruit beta testers. This recruitment process is also priming the pump, shall we say. You start the buzz by offering a limited amount of signups. People respond to exclusivity.

The best way to recruit beta testers is with a landing page. The landing page should give a brief overview of the problem the plugin solves and ask for signups. A landing page is not a tutorial or full plugin reveal. The product does not have to be ready before the landing page is launched. But, once the person signs up to be a beta tester, add them to your email marketing drip campaign about your plugin.

Wait. A Landing Page Means a Drip Campaign?

Yes. Signups to your beta testing program should be entered into a nurture (drip) campaign in your email marketing client of choice. The purpose of the drip campaign is to help your beta testers understand the problem and how your plugin provides the much-needed solution.

The welcome email should thank the user and allow them to download the zip file. Ensure the email marketing campaign asks for feedback regularly.

The emails drip out over time. They can be pre-written or published live. The point is that you keep their interest by nurturing them through the sales process. In the case of your beta testers, the sale is the download and testing. What you want from them is their feedback.

How Often Should I Email My Beta Testers?

The duration of the email depends upon your release schedule. Realistically, how long should a beta tester have to install, activate, and test out your plugin? Should it be a week or a month?

Perhaps you have the zero-day email, one the day after, the third day, the fifth, and a final email seven days later. It's okay to include a Google Form for them to fill out asking for their feedback.

After the user fills out the Google form, invite them to a private Slack Channel to freely discuss the bugs, user interface, and features with you and your team. You're showing that you value them. That will encourage them to participate.

Create A Unique Thank You Page

As a side or not-so-side-note, a thank you page after form submissions are often used sitewide. Generic thank you pages are a waste of an opportunity. You have their attention. Why not maximize this?

Include a link to one of your blog posts on object-oriented programming, flexbox guide, or even alert them to other plugins they might enjoy. Every form should have a unique thank you page. Reinforce to the user that they made the right choice.

Landing Page Checklist

- 1200 x 628 pixel Featured Image

- 155 character meta description

- Short Video

- Signup Form

- Email Marketing Campaign

- Short Pitch

- Unique Thank You Page

How Do I Promote My Landing Page?

Promote your landing page -- asking for beta testers -- on Twitter. Another great place is in your local WordPress community's group (Facebook or Slack). Share it more than once but with a different copy each time. Just sharing the link without an ask won't help.

Don't forget about large groups like Advanced WordPress on Facebook. You can find out more about this group, their code of conduct, and admins on their website at advancedwp.org. If your product is an extension of another plugin like Beaver Builder, post it in the associated plugin's Facebook Group.

You can always write personal emails to people with whom you have direct relationships. Take advantage of the personal friendships you have. If you've been helpful to others, they will most likely reciprocate.

Chapter 8

Documentation and Marketing

Documentation of your WordPress plugin is essential, not just for new users but also for future-you and the support team you'll build. You never know when your idea may scale quickly, so always prepare for the best-case scenario.

It's always easier to take notes as you're building something than to remember what you did afterward, right? Think of any meal you've made or project you've created in the woodshop. As much as you can, document your WordPress plugin alongside your development.

Documentation Is Marketing to Other Developers

The beauty of open source software is the ability to fork existing code or build extensions for existing plugins. As you build your plugin, you'll want to ensure that it can be extensible as well. Who knows? You may have the next WooCommerce on your hands.

Marketing your plugin means marketing to developers and end users. Marketing to other developers to build upon your plugin's capability means having well-written, up-to-date documentation. Just as you research your dependencies, future developers will research yours.

In open source, you will have dependencies. Your first dependency, for example, is WordPress itself. Choose your other dependencies by researching their documentation.

Read the documentation for that software, library, or API as Devin Walker recommends. If their product isn't well-documented, it could mean a major workaround for your plugin later.

> *"Documentation is very important. The thing about if I were to code a plugin and just pass it off without any documentation, a lot of people would be confused how to use it. It would take time to discover exactly what's going on. There are the regular bug fixes. Are they open to pull requests? If you need something and you want to contribute, are*

they willing to accept that or review it?"
Devin Walker (WordPress.tv and Walker)

The context of his talk was choosing third-party dependencies wisely. GiveWP used CMB2 for their plugin's UI. They moved away from that architecture around 2017 if memory serves correctly. Yes, GiveWP was forked from Easy Digital Downloads in six months. Looking back, that was the right decision then. Fast to market means fast to adoption.

Why is Documentation Important for Product Marketing?

Documentation is the source material for your copywriter. It helps them understand:

1. how your product fits in the WordPress ecosystem,

2. what problem your plugin solves,

3. and the range of applicable use-cases for your plugin.

Since your website's copywriting will be the source for email marketing, presales conversations, and social media, it's important that your copywriter has as much information as possible. Make sure your marketing team (employees or vendors) have access to your plugin's documentation. Empowering your whole team with as much information as possible will only help your team effort.

Chapter 9

Should My Plugin Be in the WordPress Plugin Directory?

The WordPress Plugin Directory is a great place to market your freemium or free WordPress plugin since it's linked to the user dashboard. The Plugin Directory used to be called the "Plugin Repository," so you may hear people referring to it like that or the "Plugin Repo."

If you choose the freemium model, hosting your plugin in the WordPress Plugin Directory helps with exposure and findability. More than 33% of your website traffic can come from WordPress.org's Plugin Directory.

You may have read some Twitter debates in the last few years about the plugin review process. This may cause hesitation, and I get it. However, listing your plugin with WordPress.org is a great way to communicate trust to WordPress users.

How Do I List My Plugin in the WordPress Plugin Directory?

WordPress.org has very specific requirements that you can read about in the developer handbook. Please refer to that.

https://wordpress.org/plugins/developers/

How Do I Optimize My Listing?

Optimizing your listing in the WordPress Plugin Directory is a specialty. Alex Denning of GetEllipsis.com does this very well. My client, Hapity.com hired him to do the same.

Use keywords that users would type in to find your product. Ensure that the image shows up well on social media. When people like your product, they'll share it.

For "Launch with Words," I signed up to use Plugin Rank[3]. Not only is it worth $9/month, but when you subscribe to their newsletter you'll get a pdf download. This guide has excellent, actionable tips that helped me optimize my readme.txt file overnight.

---

[3] This is my affiliate link for Plugin Rank. https://pluginrank.com/ref/4/

It helps that Plugin Rank's dashboard is amazing, too.

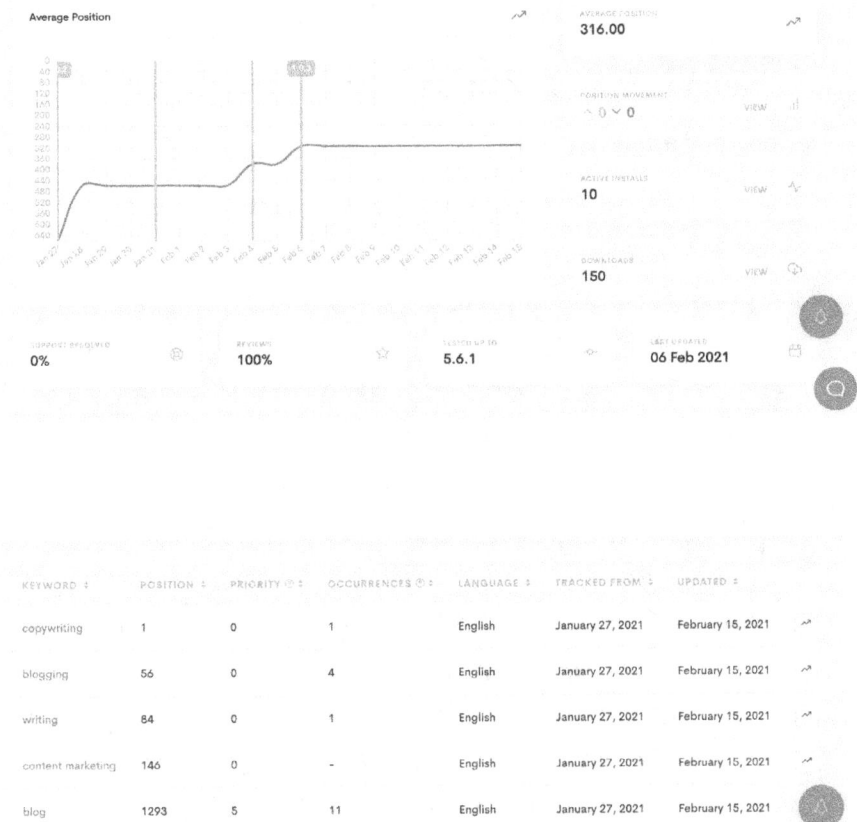

Include video, screenshots, and links to documentation on your website. Create a logo and banner and stick with that branding for the WordPress Plugin Directory. Branding carries you far. (More on creating brand guidelines is included later in the book.)

The good news, Vova Feldmen on Freemius.com reminds us, is that the algorithm behind the plugin search results is open source, which means we can optimize with intent and get results.

> "Unlike Google's super-secret-proprietary search algorithm, the WordPress.org plugin repository is an open-source project (and thanks to Daniel Iser who reminded me that yesterday and triggered this post about it). The new plugin repository is actually running on WordPress, therefore, as a derivative, it's also licensed under the GPL. This gives us a unique opportunity to simply peek under the hood of the search logic and line up the key elements developers should focus on, to rank higher on the WP.org SERP (Search Engine Result Page)." Vova Feldman (Freemius and Feldman)

Chapter 10

What Business Model is Best?

Business models and open-source seem to be opposed. But they are not, I assure you. There are three types of business models: free, premium, and freemium. To be listed in the WordPress Plugin Directory, GPL licensing is required.

Since this isn't legal advice, always talk to your attorney about trademark and licensing. Rian Kinney and ecommlegal.com are trustworthy resources.

The free business model just means people can download your plugin without charge. Your plugin is freely available in the WordPress Plugin Directory or on your GitHub repository. You can bill your users hourly for support.

The premium business model is where customers purchase your plugin from your website, and it generally includes support. The purchase is a yearly license, in most cases.

Though, some plugins often offer a limited amount of lifetime licenses.

The freemium business model is a hybrid of the two. There is a core plugin available at no charge in the WordPress Plugin Directory. You then have extensions and premium add-ons available for purchase. You may also sell packaged support options.

How Do You Finance Your Open Source Plugin?

If we're honest, open-source is funded by agency work. In many cases, the reason for the development of your plugin comes about because of client work.

GiveWP is one of the more popular plugins built as a fork of another. The agency Devin owned with a partner built quite a bit of websites for nonprofit organizations. Accepting donations online was and still is a major pain point in this industry. So, he and Matt Cromwell forked Easy Digital Downloads. He tells his story in the 2016 WordCamp Miami Talk called "Using Third Party Code to Create Unique and Meaningful Solutions." (WordPress.tv and Walker)

Jason Tucker and I interviewed Jason Coleman of Paid Memberships Pro (PMP) on Episode 149 of The Smart Marketing Show (previously called WPblab). Jason and Kim Coleman are great resources for the discussion of business models in the WordPress ecosystem.

Here is an excerpt of the show notes I wrote:

Much like the story of LifterLMS, PMP was subsidized and supported by agency work. You have to plan for your WordPress product to become self-sustaining. That plan must include profit. Make projections with a percentage and stick to it. He believes 30% profit is reasonable.

Freelancers have an advantage. When doing client work, WordPress developers are used to building something and standing by it. Not many people stand by something they have created. It's the pride in craftsmanship that is an advantage.

> A lot of freelancers move into products because they have the skill to [support something they built]." Jason Coleman (WPwatercooler Network)

Similarly, Chris Badgett told the story of LifterLMS on Episode 145 of the same podcast.

You can build your plugin quickly and finance it with client work. Be cautious of allowing client work to "cannibalize the product," as Chris describes later in the podcast.

The MVP version of the free LifterLMS was built in 90 days. codeBox always intended to move away from agency work but specialized in high-end clients and course creators. It was a natural yet intentional shift. Five years later, codeBox no longer provides agency work.

> *"It's a process; not an event. I see a product launch as the starting point, not the finish line." Chris Badgett (WPwatercooler Network)*

Chapter 11

Is a Lifetime License a Good Idea for Your WordPress Product?

You have a new WordPress product. Congratulations! Whether it is a theme or plugin, you'll most likely offer a premium license. But should it be monthly, yearly, or lifetime?

Types of WordPress Licenses

In the Open Source Software Ecosystem, there are always free licenses. Some businesses choose the freemium business model. The core plugin is free, and the upgrade comes at a price -- generally yearly. What kind of license do you offer? Is it possible to offer a lifetime license? How about charging annually or monthly?

Deciding upon pricing can be a long staff meeting. No matter what, price anchoring is a great way to show the value of the license you prefer. Price anchoring is why monthly and annual licenses exist. Most subscription services, like web hosting, offer monthly billing. Customers are familiar with it. You can pay $12 a month each month or $9 a month but billed annually. Sure, the customer can pay monthly, but it will be more costly in the long run. It looks like a deal to offer an annual price (saving $x per month), but that's the option you wanted them to buy.

Plugin developers have two lifetime options. Either you purchase one at the cost of four or five times the annual license or a limited license which is discounted. Offering a limited lifetime license is an excellent way to get users quickly. Offering a lifetime license for a limited time can help gain users at the right price point. For a new product, an active user base can be more valuable than money.

Lifetime License is a Marketing Tactic

You set up a website. You might have tweeted once or twice. How do you get users, so you hear the sweet, sweet sound of PayPal (or Stripe) notifications on your phone? There are so many ways to sell. Should you offer a lifetime license for your WordPress product?

Launching a new product in the WordPress ecosystem is not as easy as it was ten or even five years ago.

> *"Back in 2013 it was much easier to launch a WordPress theme and make it somewhat popular. Today the market for WordPress themes has become heavily crowded and oversaturated. It's near to impossible to make a theme highly successful without investing lots of time and money in marketing and building a community behind your product." Michael Hebenstreit*

WPLifetime Deals highlights all WordPress lifetime licenses currently available. These LTD licenses appeal to many users who readily share these deals when they find them. So, by offering an LTD and sharing it on social, you can get a significant rise in brand awareness. Take advantage of this in your early marketing days by filling out their contact form: https://wplifetime.deals/contact/.

Overcoming Legacy Products

New products have a few obstacles. There is the challenge to overcome the popularity of legacy products. Many times we say to ourselves, "How is anyone still using [product name]?"

The WordPress ecosystem is sixteen years old now. We've reached 35% of the market share. When searching on Google, Bing, or the WordPress.org Plugin Directory, existing products show first. They have legacy and time on their side.

There are over 54,000 plugins in the WordPress directory alone. This count does not include premium-only plugins or those who choose not to reside there. Themes are in the hundreds of thousands in the WordPress Directory. That doesn't include premium-only themes like Elegant Themes and ThemeIsle.

Overcoming the Resistance to Change

People like easy. Developers have established workflows. Agencies and freelancers use their favorite themes and plugins. They may already be using a plugin on their WordPress site that is, well, good enough. So why change?

Why should they buy your annual license? They don't even know if it's going to be better.

Offering it at a heavily discounted price helps incentivize that change. Just don't offer it at a suicide-low price.

> *"I recommend to price it as three to four-year license, to incentivize the upgrade with a decent discount." Vova Feldman (Freemius and Feldman)*

Overcoming the Affiliate Bias

Many agencies use the same old plugins over and over again because they are affiliates. Agencies and freelancers make money on the project because of the affiliate fee.

This is the reality that your new WordPress product has to overcome. Instead of free lifetime licenses, Volva Feldman suggests discounting. This helps counter the affiliate fee bias. Affiliate fees come later (90-180 days). Discounts are applied now.

> *"We give all your customers an exclusive (sic) 10% discount for our plugin! In addition, you get 10% of the revenues for the 1st year." Vova Feldman (Freemius and Feldman)*

Enter the Loss Leader

You may lose money when you offer a lifetime license for your WordPress product. But what are you gaining?

All companies offer loss leaders. For example, Ford produces a large number of Fiestas every year. That model is their loss leader. They are now doing it to change the average MPG for the EPA, but that's another issue.

> *"I sell plugins and themes as my core business, now and started off selling lifetime licenses for our plugins. However, as we found over the years, that is not a sustainable business model because you end up supporting software indefinitely and without a renewing source of income." Comment by Seth Shoultes (Post Status and Krogsgard)*

The question of a lifetime license is about acquiring customers, not financial sustainability. Your new WordPress plugin or theme may be awesome. In fact, it may be amazing! Probably, you have built it with your favorite Javascript framework. It's lightning-fast. But if no one uses it, did you even build it?

Profit and Privilege Bias

It's easy for plugin and theme developers to recommend against offering a WordPress lifetime license. This is especially true if they began early in the WordPress ecosystem. This is a privilege. It's a profit bias. Now they are in a position of profitability, and they have a certain privilege. Now, this isn't bad. They were there first. But the methods that worked for them then may not apply to 2019 and beyond.

Popular posts about the negative aspects of lifetime licenses are from established brands. We get it. With that said, those articles fail to acknowledge the unlikelihood that businesses will survive five years. The lifetime license ensures your business makes more money than if customers sign up for the annual license.

Once you make a name for yourself, you should change your pricing. Not on existing licenses, but for new customers.

> *"With our new offers, we are trying to propose an alternative to lifetime licenses with much more important economic benefits." WP Rocket (WPRocket)*

Lifetime License as Seed Money

So much of open source is funded by agencies. We have a great idea for a product or theme, and it generally comes from developers who found a solution that would work for many. It often takes up to three years for a plugin business to be self-sufficient -- if ever. So, look at the lifetime license as seed money.

I reached out to Vito Peleg from WPFeedback for his perspective. He gained $100,000 during the first 30 days of his product launch.

> *"I'm looking at lifetime deals like having a Jewish Wedding.*
>
> *When a couple gets married (or a business launches, in our case), you need some seed money to get the ball rolling and start your new life.*
>
> *Getting a surge of cash early on can be crucial to a new startup that is looking to scale and it's much easier to do with an LTD compared to building MRR or ARR when you're just starting.*
>
> *Once you secure some funds to grow, then it's time to move to the recurring model to create sustainability beyond the first few months.*

Don't undervalue your product and calculate a lifetime value of a user (yearly spend X 4.3 years) to understand your worth and start from there. It's not about getting thousands of users, it's about getting a small yet dedicated group that are willing to invest in you and give you feedback to reach 'product market fit' faster.

Remember that the more they invest the more committed they are to the success of the new product." Vito Peleg

Another argument is that you'll have too many customers to support. The truth is that a certain percentage of customers will buy it just to have it. Developers tend to stockpile plugins and domains when it's a good price. The flip side is that it is likely your customer's business won't survive five years either. This is the risk with product marketing. The better risk is seed money rather than borrowing future problems.

Lifetime License -- You Decide

This is your WordPress product. It's your child. At the end of the day, it's your decision to offer a lifetime license or not. The most important aspect to consider beyond first-year profit is optics. What kind of company and brand culture do you want to build?

> *"Grandfathered lifetime licenses are the way to go. Unfortunately, I've met my fair share of WordPress companies that refused to honour that agreement. Sadly, other than naming companies that don't grandfather your lifetime license, you are left with very little recourse." Leo Koo (WP Starters and Koo)*

Do you care about your customers? Then offer the license — limited or LTD -- keep it for your customers forever, and always give them good support. They will become raving fans. Make the offer for a limited time, like the first three to six months. Make it exclusive.

Loyalty isn't just earned. You have to maintain it. Reward your early adopters by grandfathering them in. It may be tricky with your accounting software, but it's a branding mistake not to. They are your biggest fans and most valuable test group. Reward early adopters, and they will reward you -- with word-of-mouth advertising and loyalty.

Chapter 12

What Should My Marketing Budget Be?

Marketing is an ongoing business expense. Many marketers talk about marketing as having a return or an ROI (return on investment). ROI is an accounting term that refers to assets whose value appreciates over time. Since marketing comes out of your expenses, it's not an asset. It's better to get that notion out of the way at the get-go.

Marketing is the budget that is hardest for most companies to spend because its results are generally seen in the future. Marketing results include:

- Impressions (eyeballs).

- A lift in awareness (word association).

- Affinity (how people feel about you).

- Sales.

All well-paved marketing roads lead to sales.

Impressions

Impressions are eyeballs. Think of billboards, print ads, and television or media ads. The companies selling these ad spots are paying for the potential for eyeballs to see the ad.

Scott Stratten of UnMarketing.com used to preach about the 10/10/10 rule.

At any given time, 10% of your followers are online.

Of those, only 10% will see your tweet.

Of those, only 10% (at most) will reply to your tweet.

So, if you have 700 followers, only 70 are online when you tweet. Seven will see your tweet and 1 (rounded up from 0.7) will reply.

Impressions are an opportunity.

Joe Pulizzi ✔
@JoePulizzi

Love this from @unmarketing. 10-10-10 rule of social.
10% are online. 10% of those see it. 10% of those act on
it. #DMA2012

4:24 PM · Oct 15, 2012 · Twitter for iPad

40 Retweets   **10** Likes

Awareness

Brand awareness campaigns are those that work
in the viewer's subconscious. How do you search
on the Internet? Google. What do you use to
wipe your nose? Kleenex. That word association
costs marketing dollars -- over time.

The more you're around and active where your
customers are, the more they will be aware of
you. It's more active than impressions. This is
the gateway to word-of-mouth referrals.

What's that SEO plugin? Yoast.

What's that donation plugin? GiveWP.

They're big players because they've spent their
marketing dollars to be that. Where?
WordCamps, Meetups, optimizing their plugin
directory page, hiring support staff, employees,

working on documentation, iterating the product. They both started small, just like you.

Affinity

Affinity is how people feel about your brand. When they see your logo, are they reminded of that one time they got great support? Maybe they remember the swag you gave back when we had in-person WordCamps. Think about the WordPress products you use and love. Now pick one.

How do you feel about that plugin?

_____

_____

_____

_____

_____

_____

_____

_____

_____

_____

_____

Now, how did you first hear about that plugin?

_____

_____

_____

_____

_____

_____

_____

_____

_____

_____

_____

Do you still use the plugin?

_____

_____

_____

_____

_____

_____

_____

_____

_____

_____

_____

_____

Do you recommend others use it?

_____

_____

_____

_____

_____

_____

_____

_____

_____

_____

How much money have you spent as a customer for that plugin?

_____

_____

_____

_____

_____

_____

_____

_____

_____

_____

Think about what you wrote and how you want to work that into your brand guidelines (next chapter). How do you want people to think of you?

What's a Reasonable Marketing Budget?

A reasonable marketing budget is 5% of your gross revenue, according to most sources; budget 15% of your revenue to allow faster growth. Some people market as they have extra funds. It feels extra when you are doing this with zero budget.

> "As a general rule of thumb, companies should spend around 5 percent of their total, gross revenue on marketing to maintain their current position. Companies looking to grow or gain greater market share should budget a higher percentage—usually around 10 percent." Frog Dog (Frog–Dog.com)

When you want to grow quickly, you need an unreasonable marketing budget. That is, you need one to grow. Try 15% of your gross revenue. Save that money aside for a few months. Can you hire someone to write for your website? How about a bit of help on Twitter? Can you use some of that budget to boost posts on Facebook?

Use a Budgeting Calculator

A Google Sheet is a good way to help you decide how much money to set aside. It may also help you decide how to price your Freemium product. You can fiddle around with this calculator I built. Copy it to your Google Drive.

http://bit.ly/CalcMKBudget

As you can see, if you sell 15 plugins a month at $75 each, you'll have $169 to spend on a copywriter for one blog article a month. The lowest I've seen articles going for is $100. Find someone to write for that and get your website going.

Budgeting 15% of your Gross Revenue is a good way to ensure you have the funds to hire marketing expertise so that you can keep growing.

Plugin Price	$75
Sales Per Month	15
Total Sales	**$1,125**
5%	$56
10%	$113
15%	$169

This is where it takes money to make money. Marketing is an ongoing business expense, just like your web hosting, SaaS fees, and cloud storage. It is the infrastructure you need to be in business. It's not an investment in the accounting sense that gives a return.

That is, hiring a Twitter expert won't guarantee a 4% return on your money like a life insurance policy would. One is an asset; the other is an expense.

What's the return on not marketing?

What if My Plugin is Free?

Your plugin may be free to download, but you are still asking for a sale. Unfortunately, with WordPress being as big as it is, breaking into the market will take time and effort. You will need sweat equity and/or budget.

It's best to plan to have a budget, even if you're not there yet.

Chapter 13

Create Brand Guidelines

If you have the bandwidth to create the brand guidelines yourself, then go for it. Otherwise, outsource it to someone who does these often.

At the very least, start a Google doc with your hex colors.

I have worked with Raffaella Isidori on branding guidelines when I lead the Make WordPress Marketing Team. I've also seen Jayman Pandya's work with GiveWP's guide circa 2017. Rhonda Negard takes on big clients as well. She created the brand guidelines for WPwatercooler.com as well as my site. They're all gifted professionals and amazing humans.

You'll Need a Logo Set

It is tempting to upload your plugin to the WordPress Plugin Directory without a logo (branding creative). I used to write about the most interesting new plugins. When search results showed your product without a logo (or any basic branding creatives) it didn't create much trust with me, your reviewer.

If you can't make a logo yourself, outsource it. Maybe you don't have upwards of $10,000 to spend on a complete branding package, not everyone does. Fiverr is a good resource for this. Even Canva.com has logo creation tools.

You can always use an AI service like brandcrowd.com, too. It isn't free, but it isn't $1,200 either. That's what I used for my logo for How to Get Paid Now Twitter account. It's a start.

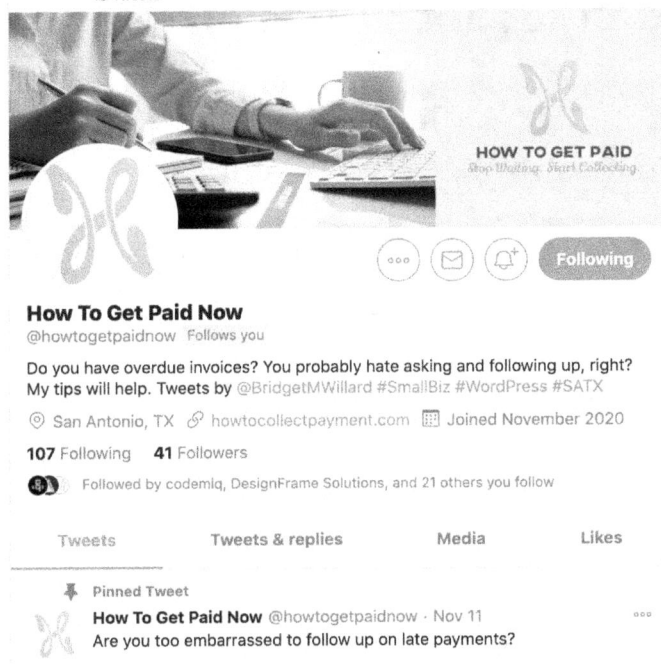

How To Get Paid Now
@howtogetpaidnow Follows you

Do you have overdue invoices? You probably hate asking and following up, right? My tips will help. Tweets by @BridgetMWillard #SmallBiz #WordPress #SATX

⊙ San Antonio, TX   🔗 howtocollectpayment.com   🗓 Joined November 2020

107 Following   **41** Followers

Followed by codemiq, DesignFrame Solutions, and 21 others you follow

| Tweets | Tweets & replies | Media | Likes |

📌 Pinned Tweet

How To Get Paid Now @howtogetpaidnow · Nov 11   ○○○
Are you too embarrassed to follow up on late payments?

You may even use the barter system with a designer you know. Get creative. Your product deserves it. Women barter with each other for services more often than you know. It's how we help each other get ahead.

You'll use your logo on your website, social media (a 500 x 500 square that fits in a circle), swag (you'll want print quality), the WordPress Plugin Directory, and probably on your 1200 x 628 featured images. If you plan on advertising, you'll need to use your logo on brand creative, too.

Brand Guidelines Checklist

- Logo Set

- Font Pairings

- Primary, Secondary, Tertiary Hex Colors

- Logo usage guidelines

- Tonality Guidelines

- Causes You Care About

About Tonality Guidelines

Do you want your company to have a personality? Of course you do. But how? One of my favorite things to do is defining something by the opposite. What do I not want?

If your plugin is financial in nature, you don't want to make jokes. Your customers need to trust you and your software with financial transactions, including their bank connections. Instead, you could decide to have a friendly yet helpful tone. You don't want to be a stuffy corporation, but you still want to be approachable.

If your plugin has a theme like a ninja, an astronaut, or even brains (I'm sure you're thinking of products here), then your tonality can match those themes. Ninjas are invisible defenders who are helpful to the community. Astronauts are strong and brave to chart a new future. Brains do all of the thinking, so you don't have to.

Rhonda Negard talks about how important it is to understand your archetype on Episode 180 of The Smart Marketing Show (WPwatercooler and Negard).

> *"So one of my clients, she's a resume and LinkedIn writer, so she will help you find help you rewrite your LinkedIn profile, so that you get that dream job. Or rebrand or rewrite your resume so that you get the interview and can get your dream job. When she took it, her archetype is the Joker. And, you know, some people might cringe oh my gosh, do I really want a joker archetype? Working on my resume, how I make money, how I'm paying all the bills, you know, this is my reputation. And I really want my dream job. Well, there are ways to do that. So you also have tendencies. So you have these great qualities that you can have as whatever your*

archetype is, the Joker doesn't take themselves too seriously. It's more about fun and entertainment, right? But that can go negative. And you can look like you're flippant, you know? Like maybe you're a little bit of a trickster kind of thing. And you don't want to do that. So, when we talked about it, we don't want her brand to have all kinds of crazy typography and certainly not some crazy wild color palette either. She needs to be a little grounded. But what she can do is go for the angle, like, Okay, I'm 35 years old, and I was just laid off from my job, I do not want to go move back in with mom and dad. So you can play on that."

Causes You Care About

As part of your brand guidelines, it is a good thought exercise to identify one to five causes that you are passionate about. Do any of these causes align with your mission and your brand's voice?

When they do, co-marketing with the cause is a great way to give back to the world and raise brand awareness.

Chapter 14

You Are Not Your Audience

If we only had a dollar for every time we've heard, "you are not your audience," we would be hundredaires. Seriously, though, we tend to forget this -- especially as plugin downloads increase.

Our original audience may be our peers, but as our user base tells others and our brand awareness campaigns start to work, you won't completely know who your audience is.

But you told me to get beta testers from my peer group, you may be wondering. This is true. When you're building and testing your plugin, you are your audience to some degree. As sales increase and word of mouth has an effect, you'll start to learn that people like your product.

Success has a way of distancing us from our audience; it's neither good nor bad. It just is. Finding ways to understand our new customers, how they found our product, and why they're using it is so important. Short surveys, phone calls, and even conversations on Twitter are great ways to build your database of user stories.

That kind of consumer insight is marketing gold. We can create advertising campaigns, build extensions and add feature sets, and scale sales from this information.

Do I Need a Persona Doc?

Whether or not you need a formal document outlining your personas is up to you. You can decide that you have "Bob The Web Developer," "Mary the Church Secretary," and "Larry the Agency Owner" and assign them values and even archetypes as Rhonda Negard suggests.

As your plugin shop grows, this may be helpful. For now, maybe start a Google Doc noting the type of people who purchase your plugin. Or download a CSV from Easy Digital Downloads and import it into Google Sheets.

Surveys can help you determine what each of these people like and how they self-identify. Remember, however, that people are alive. Meaning they grow and change. As they grow and change, their tastes grow and change.

"Bob The Web Developer" may have started by liking IPAs in his twenties but now prefers a good Argentinian Malbec with his steak.

Personas are stereotypes. Use social listening to keep them up to date.

Chapter 15

Accounting for Affiliates

Affiliate marketing in the WordPress ecosystem is popular among both product owners and WordPress developers and agencies. With that in mind, you'll want to factor in whom you would like to be an affiliate, how you will implement the system, and factor it into your pricing model.

> *"With the channel-based marketing philosophy, it's easy to filter these opportunities: if something fits with the channel you're focusing on, do it. If not, don't do it." Alex Denning (Denning)*

Who Should Be An Affiliate?

Every person who signs up to be an affiliate and is approved is an extension of your brand. It's tempting to go after the big names and keynote speakers. However, they may not be the right demographic for your WordPress plugin.

So how do you know if an affiliate aligns with your brand? This is where your brand guidelines come in. Along with your affiliate application, you may want to do a bit of research as well. You wouldn't want someone to have conflicting messaging because that can muddy your marketing waters. Think about how it will look and make your best decision. It's not a life or death decision, but it may make you feel a bit awkward.

How Do I Implement Affiliate Marketing?

There are quite a few services that help you manage and implement affiliate marketing. Ninja Forms and Pressable use Share A Sale. Beaver Builder's forms are on their own site, and payments come through PayPal. Thrive Cart is used by WP Agency Summit.

The best way to implement, in many respects, depends upon your revenue model and business goals. It's not a bad idea to reach out to plugins you know who have already created a system that works for them. Ask them what they use, why it works, and what they'd use if they were starting now.

If you're polite, most WordPress professionals are completely willing to tell you their story.

Accounting for Affiliate Marketing

WordPress developers know how to get things to work -- this includes getting the best pricing. So, when you offer an affiliate marketing program, be sure to account for that discount and possibly create an agreement that doesn't allow the affiliate to purchase for themselves.

For example, Beaver Builder's Affiliate Agreement states:

> "*May not be purchased by Affiliate, an already-existing partner or other affiliate of the Company;*" (Beaver Builder)

If your plugin is $400 and that's priced on you barely making a profit, you won't want to lose 20% every time it's used. Instead, bump up the price accordingly. This is how you account for affiliate marketing without going negative. That's never a good thing.

Most agencies and developers sign up to be an affiliate and give that link to their clients to purchase the plugins needed for their website. With the affiliate revenue, they make a bit more money on their website build. I'd argue that many freelancers should charge more, but that's another book.

Chapter 16

Social Media Overview

Social media is the ability to interact with people online. Geographical and social barriers almost disappear. Those brands that leverage social media can gain a significant advantage over more prominent brands that do not.

The consistent, public use of social media with the intent of building relationships and sharing knowledge is your best friend. Remember that it is a long game and not an instant fix. So many businesses (in and outside of WordPress) turn to social media to save their business. It isn't the last resort; it's the first step.

What's The Best Social Media Platform?

The best social media platform is the one you use -- consistently. With that said, for most WordPress products, the best platform is Twitter. Your primary audience will be other developers who spend time on Twitter. It's also good to note that Google indexes tweets. They're a strong social signal for SEO.

LinkedIn is another great network for WordPress professionals who are going after the C-Suite audience. Having an active role there is vital since you'll most likely also engage do-it-yourselfers and website implementers. Though you can create a Company Page on LinkedIn and post there, you will not interact with your page's home feed. This is a point of frustration and a reminder that you as an individual are the best representation of your brand.

Facebook Pages are good for the social signals for Google ranking, middle-market people, and beginners. Where Facebook Pages shine is in boosted and promoted posts to specific audiences, you can make $20 go pretty far when you start testing audiences.

Using Google Analytics and correlating social referrals with time on page will give you a good idea of who is reading. But remember this -- people will read your blog posts on Twitter (high time on site) but most likely go to your site (root) to purchase. The conversions may all be direct. This is where hard data gets a little less black and white.

You also won't necessarily be able to account for those users who surf the web in Incognito or Private Mode.

Do I Need Video?

Videos (explainer videos, tutorials, and even webinars or interviews) are always helpful content to host and share online. This content can be transcribed, subtitled, and repurposed on your company's blog. Editing the transcript into blog format is an easy way to meet your publishing goals.

I recommend uploading your videos to YouTube since it's the second largest search engine. Be sure to include transcripts. The internet is blind. Search engines index those transcripts. I use Temi.com for my videos which is the AI branch of Rev.com. Jason Tucker uses Otter.ai for transcripts on the WPwatercooler Network.

Though the block editor now allows transcripts for video in your WordPress media library, video can slow down your server and create storage issues. Wistia and Vimeo are other video hosting services and have great embedding features for hosting private videos. However, to create another way for people to find your product and purchase it, YouTube is the way to go. You can use Vimeo for private videos and YouTube for front-facing videos. That's a win-win!

Should I Hire an Intern?

I would be wary of hiring an intern in general. There are labor laws in many states against using an intern as free labor. With that said, an intern is an inexperienced, low-wage employee with a limited time of employment.

Do you want an inexperienced person representing your brand online? Making a mistake as a brand online is rare but not easy to come back from. If you plan on overseeing the intern and approving things before they are posted, then the risk is mitigated.

Also, be careful about humor. You won't want to make Boomer jokes if that's your audience, for example.

You may purchase my book "**Keys to Being Social**" on Amazon.com for in-depth insight and examples on how to be effective on social media.

Chapter 17

Represent Your Product by Attending Meetups and WordCamps

Automations, funnels, and drip campaigns have their place in marketing. Marketers love to talk about these tools along with how to optimize this, that, and the other thing. Regardless of the tools you decide to use, the best system is showing up.

The Art of Showing Up

The best way to build brand awareness is face time with your target audience. For WordPress plugins, this means attending local Meetups and WordCamps. When I first began regularly attending WordPress Meetups in 2016, I noticed that Gregg Franklin, the Marketing Manager of ServerPress, was always there.

Gregg models this behavior beautifully. Of course, he talks about DesktopServer and WPSiteSync when appropriate, but more importantly, he attends to give. The ServerPress team has consistently shown up at their local Meetups and traveled to WordCamps near and far.

It's important to look at your schedule and see where you can fit a Meetup in -- even if it's virtual. In some ways, the COVID-19 pandemic has made it easier to attend virtual WordPress Meetups and WordCamps.

Speak at Meetups and WordCamps

WordCamps are the celebration of what the local community has done during the year. They're the regional event for all things WordPress. It's great to attend, be in the sessions, meet people, talk to sponsors, and send out some tweets.

One way to increase your brand awareness is to speak at these events. The first step to speaking is applying. If we go back a step, you can present at your local Meetup. That's a great way to test the waters if you're not used to speaking. Should you apply to speak? Yes. The worst-case scenario is that your talk isn't accepted. But if you don't apply, you say "no" to yourself. Say "yes" to yourself.

Speaking may feel uncomfortable to you. You may have a bit of anxiety. But I promise that you have something valuable to share. The audience will have an opportunity to get to know you as a person. Though you are not allowed to pitch your product from the stage, pairing your WordCamp talk with tweets during, before, and after the conference will help your brand awareness. Product sales will follow.

If you are totally opposed to speaking, you can always sponsor a person who is comfortable speaking to represent your brand. As with your affiliates, you'll want to ensure their brand aligns with yours. Companies offer honorariums from $300 for sponsored speakers. Travel and lodging may even be included.

Chapter 18

Sponsoring WordCamps

Whether you decide to sponsor at the highest tier and staff a booth or at a lower tier, sponsoring a WordCamp is more than just giving back. This is a use of your marketing budget.

Funding Your Sponsorship

With hotel and airfare costs included, it costs around $1,000 per person to travel to a WordCamp. So, let's say you and one other person staff your booth -- two is best. That's $2,000.

Sponsoring a table (booth) at a WordCamp can run upwards of $1,500 depending upon how large the camp is. Let's go with $2,000. Then you will want swag. Let's give a budget of $500.

This WordCamp is now at $4,500 of your marketing budget.

With the 15% of gross revenue benchmark, you'd have to sell 400 of your $75 licenses to have the marketing budget to sponsor a WordCamp at this level.

This is entirely achievable; I recommend you do this in the first quarter of Year 3 (See Add-on 1). You can always attend and speak at WordCamps within driving distance or offer a small speaker sponsorship until you're ready to sponsor a booth.

Plugin Price	$75
Number of Sales	400
Total Sales	**$30,000**

5%	$1,500
10%	$3,000
15%	$4,500

Staffing a Sponsor Table

Staffing a sponsor table at a WordCamp can be overwhelming for those new to the community or even just new to standing all day.

Prepare Your Event Team

Prepare your team way ahead, so they know what to expect. When will they be allowed to attend sessions, if any? Who will cover lunch, or will your booth be closed? Who brings the swag? What time should your staff members arrive and how late are they expected to stay? Is this part of their paid salary or a gift to the community?

The first thing to remember is that this is a WordCamp, not a mall at a kiosk. Being aggressive does not work.

Prepare Before WordCamp

One to two weeks ahead, look at the attendees' page to get an idea of who will be there. Follow the hashtag on Twitter and reply to people who are excited about the camp.

Some things you can say are:

- See you there.

- Do you have any tips for this city?

- What session are you looking forward to?

Tips During WordCamp

- Arrive early. Usually, tables are first come, first served.

- Put out your swag in a way that is visually appealing.

- You probably don't need to save too much swag for day 2. There's a 50-25% drop off in attendance.

- Tweet out a selfie saying you are there and asking people to say hi. Use the WordCamp hashtag, not their Twitter handle. Remember, if you start a tweet with an @ handle, it is considered a reply. You want to avoid that. Use a period first to trick Twitter.

- Stand up. People won't talk to you if you're sitting down. This is especially true if you are looking at your phone/computer.

- If you need a break, go into a session and tweet from there. Learn. Take notes. Absorb. You should be able to learn at least one thing.

- If one of your teammates is speaking, definitely support them.

    - Smile. It's hard. I know. But it helps.

    - Ask people questions. Don't ask about your service or product (yet). This gets people talking. Get insight from your audience.

        - How do you use WordPress?

        - What has been your favorite session so far?

        - What did you get for lunch?

    - Tweet selfies with your booth attendees. If someone won a prize, definitely tweet that, too.

    - Take notes. It's fine if it's just bullets. Your supervisor may ask you for insights from the camp. This makes it much easier to remember things.

Examples

Bluehost ✓
@bluehost

We are here at #WCOC this weekend in sunny California! ☀️ 🌴 Stop by our booth, grab some swag...and pick up a copy of the #BluehostBlueprint. 😎

1:44 PM · Apr 27, 2019

♡ 17   See Bluehost's other Tweets

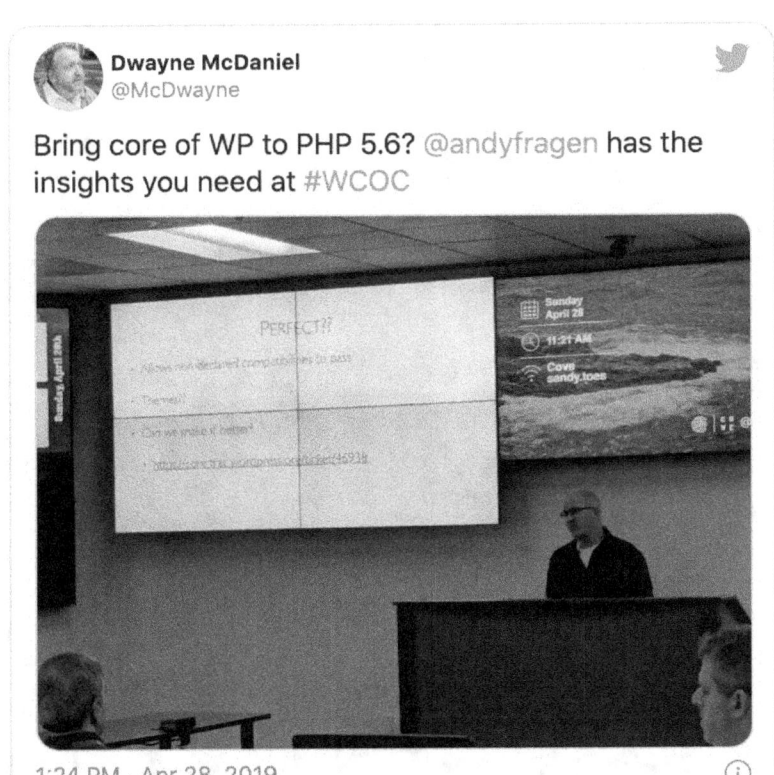

Dwayne McDaniel
@McDwayne

Bring core of WP to PHP 5.6? @andyfragen has the insights you need at #WCOC

1:24 PM · Apr 28, 2019

♡ 3   See Dwayne McDaniel's other Tweets

Bre McDede
@breannmcdede

My other awesome teammate @0aveRyan giving his
talk Take Command With Custom WP-CLI Commands
#WCOC @bluehost

1:57 PM · Apr 28, 2019   ⓘ

♡ 11   ⚇ See Bre McDede's other Tweets

Pressable
@Pressable

Just hanging out with @postphotos from @XWP — as you do. #WCOC

2:09 PM · Apr 28, 2019   ⓘ

♡ 15   See Pressable's other Tweets

12:02 PM · Apr 27, 2019

Chapter 19

Nonprofits and Hackathons

Volunteering for a nonprofit or participating in a hackathon is a wonderful way to give back. Not only do you help a nonprofit with its website, but you get to meet like-minded folks. If you're part of a volunteer team, you can also make friends in that space. Forming a business relationship with those who care about the same causes that you do is never a bad thing -- especially when it comes to marketing.

Which causes should you help?

Think about the nonprofits you listed in your brand guidelines. Do any of them need a bit of help with their website? Is your plugin a good fit for their fundraising or marketing goals? Why not reach out? Send them an email introducing yourself. Better yet, pick up the phone and call them.

I cannot help a nonprofit necessarily with website building, for example, but I can donate. As part of my mission to empower others, I am a recurring donor to the World Wildlife

Foundation, the National Domestic Violence Hotline, FreeCodeCamp, United Christian Ministries, Oxfam, The Ocean Institute, and the Nature Conservancy. In all those small monthly donations are 18% of my profit.

With my time, I continue to work with Make WordPress, most recently with the 'needs copy review' tag in WordPress Core Trac. I also donated one hour of consulting to a WordPress professional each month in 2020.

Get creative. There are ways you can help even if they're not a 501(c)3 tax write-off. It's always going to help with brand awareness. This is why Sport Clips works with St. Jude's Children's Research Hospital. It's important to their organization as a whole.

Participate in Hackathons

GiveCamp.org puts together teams during a weekend where you can meet other folks like you, help a nonprofit, and have some fun. DoAction.org and 48in48.org are also national events that are fantastic to be part of. Your local WordPress or Javascript Meetup may also organize a hackathon or volunteer event.

"It's important to give back and to put back into your local community. I think you feel a little bit of ownership in the continued success of that organization. And I think more people would give more or participate in things like this knowing that's one of the takeaways in this and the time commitment is relatively short." Alex J Vasquez (Vasquez)

In 2016 while I was working with GiveWP, we donated licenses to Website Weekend LA. Natalie MacLees and Alex Vasquez organized this local hackathon. As a team, we felt really good about participating in this cause. Even better is that GiveWP gained customers for a lot longer than a license. As part of the plugin's mission of "democratizing donations," participating in this event made sense. It aligned with our core values. Donating licenses is an action that aligns with those values.

Nonprofits and Content Marketing

A small way you can support your chosen nonprofit is through your content marketing. Make it a point to mention them on your website and why you've chosen them. Since that cause aligns with your values, you're sure to attract customers who believe in that, too!

Sharing articles and tweets from that cause gives you more content for your social media campaigns, too!

Chapter 20

Scaling Will Increase Support Tickets

What comes with success is scale. Scale means more sales, and more sales mean more support tickets. If your documentation has missing information, you'll get more support tickets. If your documentation is hard to find, you'll get more support tickets. If your sales copy promises something that your product doesn't deliver, you'll get more support tickets.

Once you feel that your support tickets are rolling in too quickly, it may be a good time to have a third party audit your documentation to prevent unnecessary support tickets. Brainstorm with your content marketing team to address frequently appearing questions in blog content. When you start to feel that you have no ideas on blogging topics, the support queue is an excellent raw material resource.

Since this book isn't about the whole business of selling a plugin, I'm not going to delve into support. Also, there's no point in reinventing the wheel. Matt Cromwell and Team Give wrote the "The GiveWP Support Manual" available on their GitHub repo. Check it out, fork it, send them a Thank You Tweet and take what works for you.

Chapter 21

It's Totally Normal to Market In Phases

When you've created something and are about to launch it, the excitement is almost intoxicating. You're relieved, nervous, and anxious. It's an amazing thing, truly.

You may feel pressure to copy tactics that the "big guys" or established plugin shops. Remember that they have already built their brand awareness and product catalog. They've gone through the first three years of marketing their products. Most successful plugin developers would do something different had they started again.

With that said, the strategy and tactics that worked for them in 2003, 2004, and even 2010 won't necessarily work today. The market is different today. The market matures, grows, and evolves.

"When we launched Pagely in 2009 we had the market all to ourselves, a blue ocean. Within a few years, there were a dozen or so

competitors all saying the same things. Many of them were massive companies moving into the space, or well funded VC backed companies hellbent on growth at all costs. In this very, very red ocean, we had to ask ourselves how we were going to survive as a revenue-funded small team.

We elected to seek open water and over the course of a few years we re-positioned our brand, revamped our service, and began to target a different segment of the widening channel. We left the volume driven B2C segment to everyone else and focused on the needs of value-driven B2B, higher education, media, and enterprise companies with a flexible and high-touch approach. That kicked off a multiyear run of growth for our company and most likely saved us from sputtering out." Joshua Strebel (Pagely.com and Strebel)

Though your market may be a big, open blue ocean, WordPress itself is not a blue ocean. It's full of plugins, tens of thousands of plugins. Your tactics need to be different.

Developing and Marketing In Phases

Just as you develop your product in phases, you'll want to roll out your marketing slowly. Developing and marketing in stages goes together like peanut butter and jelly or peanut butter and hagelslag. You get it.

> *"Skilled product marketers shape the curve: speeding through the Introduction, increasing the slope of the Growth phase, extending the length of Maturity, and easing the pace of the Decline." Derek Gleason (CX Optimization Agency)*

A phased launch (beta, version 1, iteration, version 2, etc.) is a non-threatening way to improve your product. As customers use your plugin, they will give feedback. Knowing you're not your audience means there will be use cases you didn't think of.

Support tickets will give you ideas for the next iteration. You'll see tweets from people who love the plugin. People will ask questions on your contact form.

Phased Marketing Outside of WordPress

Restaurants and galleries have soft launches before their grand opening. What worked? What didn't work? Were the hors d'oeuvres right for the gallery, or was it messy to clean up? How did the lighting go?

The automobile industry phases marketing and development with their concept cars. With development, they begin with a sketch and get buy-in. If it's approved, they will make a full-size clay model. The next phase includes a build and taking it to auto shows. Will it ever hit the factory floor? If it does, it will be a modified version.

> *"If we have a new launch of a new version in our portfolio, we would tease that with a specific type of concept that would be a slight exaggeration of the production car." David Woodhouse, Design Director Lincoln Motor Company (Business Insider and Caldwell)*

This concept car is marketed at each phase. You see the sketches in magazines -- online and print. You'll see TV ads, write-ups, commercials. Now, you'll see their marketing on social media. They hit the auto shows and then decide to take it to production. Then it's a full-out assault.

Some of us have been waiting for the "new" VW Bus since 2001. They came out with another concept in 2011. Then again in 2016 and 2017. At this point, I'm dubious it will ever hit the factory floor. But that's the point of the marketing. Test out what the market wants. Is it feasible? Can you hit the EPA's guidelines on MPG? Will it be cost-effective? Do you have the ability to produce this vehicle?

So the cycle is idea, market, build, launch, market, iterate, launch. You can apply this method to your plugin development with your versions. Plan out your roadmap. What is a reasonable amount of time between releases?

Development and WordPress Core Updates

WordPress Core has three to four major releases each year. In 2021, there will be four[4] core updates. Each core update will have an alpha, beta, and release candidate. There will be two

---

[4] At the time of this writing there were four updates planned for 2021. That roadmap has since changed to three. WordPress 5.8 will ship in July of 2021 and 5.9 in December 2021.

weeks between the launch and the release candidate. You may want to consider their schedule when you create your development roadmap.

Chapter 22

Discounts and Rice Christians

For fifteen years, starting in 2001, my late husband and I started a ministry with a few friends. Our mission was to help the homeless in Anaheim -- those who were on the streets and motels. We had a controversial approach to our outreach. We provided a hot meal and toiletries before we ever spoke about the Bible.

In mainline Christianity and missions, the people we are meant to reach (our demographic) are often asked to listen to our preaching. Then, and only then, would we give them sustenance -- "rice."

For fundraising purposes, this was amazing. Churches were full. Tents in fields were full. People were accepting Jesus and converting to Christianity. Wow. It's amazing.

What happens when the missionary leaves or the funds dry up? The missionary team doesn't provide rice and loses a majority of their congregation. We refer to these people, who convert for a meal, "Rice Christians." In the end, they came to get what they needed; there is no loyalty.

So, yes, the approach we took as a ministry was different. We never required anyone to attend a church meeting to meet their physical needs.

We'd go back to our home church on Sunday and tell our stories, write about them on our blog, and donors were so excited about changed lives. Then, the holidays would roll around, and donors came out to see what we were doing.

It was always on a Friday night, generally outside in a parking lot. In the winter, it was pretty cold just to stand around outside. We were happy to serve a meal and chat with everyone. Then, we would circle up around the pastor to hear the sermon. Some people would inevitably leave at this time.

"Why are people leaving?" they would ask us after the Thanksgiving meal. Some people needed to find shelter before it got too dark. Others had to go to a shelter or their half-way home before curfew. And still others would stand at the outside of the circle, sort of lurking. They were there. They were listening. Months would pass, and soon they were closer and closer to our circle until they were part of it.

Marketing, like mission work, is a long-term endeavour. If you look for short-term results, like photo opportunities or mailing list signups, you'll be disappointed in the end. They signed up for your email list to get the discount code. Once they made the purchase, they unsubscribe and you're back to square one.

Discounts Don't Encourage Loyalty

Discounts are great. Everyone loves to use a discount. It's tempting to offer a discount as an incentive to get an email subscriber. Discounts may help with one sale (conversion), but they won't necessarily produce loyalty. However, when you're selling annual licenses, you want a lifetime customer, not just a right-now customer.

> *"Discounts are not a win-win. Customers may be drawn in and business may boom, but it's very short lived. The conversions come at high costs and retention is basically non-existent. eCommerce has been democratized by discount giants like eBay*

and Amazon. Consumers are increasingly comparison shopping, even while they are instore." (Annex Cloud and Ogino)

Positive Reinforcement and Loyalty

Positive reinforcement is a great way to build a relationship which is the path to loyalty. Loyalty, whether in a family, friendship, relationship, or with a brand, has to be earned and maintained. Relationships break down when loyalty isn't maintained. So, focus on creating a loyalty program instead.

> *"The best way to influence customer behavior with positive reinforcement is by using a 'continuous' reinforcement schedule with loyalty rewards. This is where the user is rewarded each time they complete a specified action, as opposed to being rewarded at fixed intervals (ie. every month or every year). For example, by delivering a reward every time a customer makes a successful referral, they will learn to associate referrals with a positive outcome and likely repeat the behavior."*
> *(SaaSquatch)*

Even small things like stickers and exclusive swag, not available at WordCamps, are a great way to show your customers that they matter -- especially agency customers.

Paying attention to your super fans on Twitter with this in mind is another way to encourage loyalty. You can list them as "Super Fans;" they'll be notified and get a bit of a dopamine from the notification. This group of people may also be the perfect place to recruit guest bloggers and use cases. The people who are already willing to talk about you online are your influencers.

Chapter 23

How Do I Approach Content Marketing?

Content marketing uses articles from your blog across social media and email marketing to bring customers to your online store. By regularly publishing helpful content to your audience, you will gain and retain more customers.

My content marketing strategy is always education-focused. Help people understand more about the subject matter with the mindset that you provide the solution.

While scrolling on Twitter, it's unlikely your brand will be recognized, let alone get a first-click lead. Meaning, it's doubtful they will see a tweet, not knowing your product, click it and purchase right then. First-click leads are like the Abominable Snowmen of marketing analytics. In truth, people search, hear about your product, and buy it.

Your published content should align with your brand, be helpful, and invite customers to engage with you.

Publishing on Your Company Blog

We've talked about the "one site to rule them all" philosophy previously. You have one company website with several product pages (when you grow your plugin base) and one blog to rule them all.

Commit to publishing once a month at first; this will take about two hours total. You don't have to be a rockstar writer or reporter on WPTavern. Think about questions your market demographic may have for their business or organization. Writing about these tangents is a great way to market your plugin. Remember that your blog is for your users, not you. Developers may see your blog post but will more likely go to your documentation for what they need.

Publishing regularly does a few things for your brand awareness. Firstly, it is a ranking signal for Google and other search engines. (You're in business and you're not going anywhere.) Secondly, it gives you something to share on social media that isn't a hard sell. (Hello

Twitter!) In addition, it creates a way for people to learn from your brand and form a bond with your company. (Affinity is awesome.) Being helpful is a powerful way to gain loyalty. Affinity leads to loyalty; loyalty leads to sales.

If your plugin is for nonprofits like GiveWP, write a series of articles on how nonprofits can use each platform. That's one of many ideas we implemented. LifterLMS has great articles for course creators that help them with production and marketing. Ninja Forms writes about connecting to your CRM and lead generation tips for small businesses.

The market is nonprofits. The tangent is nonprofit marketing. Write about that.

The market is course creators. The tangent is marketing for memberships. Write about that.

The market is for small businesses. The tangent is getting leads. Write about that.

Email Marketing and Nurture Campaigns

Email marketing is a critical way to follow up with the people who found your site, product, article and want to know more. Whether you automate your campaign or send it out manually, this is how you nurture leads.

Drip campaigns are sent out at specific intervals. It may be that the email is sent when they sign up and every week after. I've done this with both of my book's drip campaigns. There is a welcome email for this book, and then every email is sent at 10:00 am each Tuesday. The newest subscribers start at the first email and go forward.

Drip campaigns are great for teaching people how to use your plugin. Including them after purchase and educating your customers will also help reduce support requests. We love that! Last year, I edited the drip campaign for PeepSo. It's a guide to all things community for the new user. They opted for a daily campaign over 25 days. It's brilliant!

Nurture campaigns are nudging a potential customer toward a sale. Cart abandonment emails do something very similar as well. Mailchimp partner and expert Amy Hall explains this beautifully.

> *"A nurture campaign is based on a potential customer's behavior. For example, if a person clicks a link that takes them to a free*

download, the download triggers a second email that thanks them for downloading. Then it suggests the next step the person can take. If, however, the person does not download, an email to remind them to download may be sent.

With a nurture campaign, each email is designed to bring the person ever closer to making a purchase. It requires more thought and behavior analysis, but it's targeted toward individuals on your list who are actually interacting and moving closer to doing what you want them to do, purchase." (Hall)

Email marketing should have a purpose and a single call to action. It's tempting to put your whole newsletter in the campaign, but it's too much. No one wants to read that. You also don't want to bug someone every single day (I'm looking at you, Old Navy) or only once a year at Black Friday.

If you publish a blog post once a month, aim for an email marketing campaign for a couple days later to send out the post. The call to action is "read the article." Make it simple and ensure that you have as few images as possible. Most people have images turned off.

Now, just because someone opens your email doesn't mean they're ready to buy (click) either. So many people save an email for later. For example, they may see the email on their phone but read it later from their desktop. This is common in the WordPress ecosystem.

Social Media and Content Marketing

Social media is a great place to share your content but it's also a fantastic place to nurture potential customers and curate content from other people. Approach Twitter like the hallway track at a WordCamp. Be fun, casual, and friendly. Don't be afraid to start a conversation by replying to a tweet.

Following others shows you are interested in other people. This is true leadership. In addition, you will forge friendships, nurture affinity, and learn along the way.

Facebook Pages are great for boosting posts and testing audiences. Though with data and privacy laws constantly changing, some posts will serve better than others. As an insider tip, ensure that your blog or landing page's featured image is 1200 x 628 pixels with less than 20% of the space covered in words. Though Facebook claims that they have removed this rule, I'm wary of trusting them.

LinkedIn is professional and the culture allows for bragging. This is a great place to talk about your latest customer review, active install counts, and personal achievements. Though you can and should set up a company page, you cannot interact in the home feed with your page. People want to be connected to you as a human. Be that person and you'll win.

So should you start a Facebook Group?

I'm not so sure that starting a Facebook Group is the best play, especially in the first two years. It seems to me from all of my stalking that Facebook Groups in WordPress tend to be places for support. It may seem like that helps take it off of your company's shoulders, but I'd ask for you to think about it differently.

Do you want to sponsor a group which you do not have time to participate in? It will have your brand with a bunch of people complaining about this, that, and something else they don't like. It's asking for trouble. Keep your support in support where it belongs and spend that time nurturing your customer base on Twitter. It really is the best use of your time. I promise.

Chapter 24

When Developing Your Plugin Isn't Fun Anymore

Once your plugin becomes successful to the point that you don't recognize the audience, you may not even like your product anymore. Not to say that you're not proud of it, but it doesn't captivate your interest as much. You may be tempted to move on to the next project. Your pre-sales questions, support tickets, and followers online will tell you that your product is necessary. It is useful.

To you, your product may have lost its original luster. That's fine. It doesn't mean that you should move on. This is the fork in the road. This is your opportunity to double down on your product. This is when you double down on yourself.

If you partnered with a business manager, you've likely had this conversation. It's hard to stay interested in a project when it feels finished and/or becomes "work." So, how do you keep going?

How Do You Know If You Should Keep Developing?

I asked a few of my friends who are long-term plugin developers for their advice. I am hoping their advice brings you the encouragement you need when you feel like giving up.

Your product is worth putting out into the world, friend.

"After working on anything for a long time, be it a degree, website, or plugin, there will undoubtedly be times when you feel fatigue. Your relationship with your code is like a relationship in real life: it can be a lot of work.

Why not try something new? Isn't that what they say in couples therapy? But hey, the same works for me and my codebase!

I get new ideas on my own, from our team, as well as our users. Make sure you're using a service like Canny.io to gather feedback and grow a community on social media to give you valuable insights.

I like to start my ideas with a combination of design and text explaining the features and functionality. You may prefer another method and it's totally up to you. Just get your idea out! Once I'm relatively confident in it, I like to gather feedback internally and often present it to our community for more feedback.

If you need a quick win, spruce up an outdated interface with some quick design updates. You don't have to jump right into a big batch item.

Sometimes nothing's better than a quick feeling of accomplishment!" **Devin Walker**, Founder & CEO of GiveWP

"The LifterLMS plugin project is over 6 years old as of this writing. It's not always fun, but we are just getting started.

What makes this mindset and unstoppable momentum possible?

Our mission to democratize education in the digital classroom contributes to the momentum. There are teachers, trainers and coaches, education entrepreneurs we call *them, all over the world that use our plugin to build learning platforms that can reach the entire world. We believe in these education entrepreneurs, and they're counting on us. Online learning opportunities hold the power to change individuals, communities, and the world for the better. A service mindset to these education entrepreneurs carries us through.*

We're also on a mission to be a model for how to do freemium in WordPress. We give away more for free than most, yet still have a very viable business. We lead by example here and this freemium business model leadership mission motivates us as well.

On a more inward level, I am incredibly loyal to my cofounder and our team of hard working smart team members (and their families). The plugin business has created incredible income and lifestyle freedoms that we've grown accustomed to. It's kind of like the military where a soldier has this loyalty to the fellow soldier, especially in combat, and would do anything to protect them.

So when the going gets rough, the company mission and the loyalty to your team members will carry you through. This *highlights the importance of working with passion on a business that improves the world in some way with great people that care about each other beyond simply being transactional business colleagues." **Chris Badgett,** Founder & CEO of LifterLMS*

"I find renewed interest in my product when I have to explain PMPro to a peer, advisor, and even family or friends. The simple act of explaining my plugin to someone new helps me see the product through a new set of eyes.

We also make an effort to talk to our longest term customers. As your product grows, a founder naturally becomes more removed from the end user. You have a team now. They answer support tickets, operate presales channels, and manage user accounts.

Dive back into direct conversations with your customer.

• Listen to their positive feedback

• *Learn how your product has improved their business or life*

• *Take their pain points seriously.*

Founders tend to front load the product development process with these conversations and abandon them once established and profitable." **Kim Coleman, Co-founder Paid Memberships Pro**

"*In answer to your question as to whether or not we should keep developing, the answer is simple: As long as there is demand, we'll keep developing.*

As far as how do we keep ourselves motivated? I will grant you that sometimes that can be hard. When we find ourselves getting in a rut either collectively or individually, we run an exercise where we work to see the product through our customers' eyes; whether they are seasoned fans, or newbies. Talking to them, looking at the emails they send us with their thoughts, looking at testimonials goes a long way. Before COVID, I made it a point to make sure that every one of our team interacted with the Community at some level. WordCamps are always the best. Developers ESPECIALLY need to hear what people think of what they're doing because they spend so much time debugging code that they gaslight themselves into believing their product is garbage. In reality, they're not looking at the 999,999 things that work right because they're too busy wrapped up in that 1 thing that isn't. Work on that one thing long enough and that, in their mind, becomes what their product is. When they talk to people who use their product, it always gets them out of that funk and motivates them to work harder on it." **Marc Benzakein,** *Operations Manager of ServerPress LLC*

"Bring someone new as a product owner (or other key roles). A new team member will bring new energy and perspective, which will help to push things forward. If you are an agency like Multidots where our investment in the plugin is developers time, it becomes more tempting to lose interest as there is no real money to lose. Therefore, if I started a plugin and didn't launch it, I'll pay back in cash to my company for the developer's time

in the plugin — this commitment to payback has been a strong push to bring the plugin to the finish line. If you have made any "revenue or download" projection plan during the planning phase, I will review it for more encouragements; because that's why you started it in the first place, right?" **Anil Gupta**, CEO & Co-Founder of Multidots

Add-on 1

Three Year Plugin Marketing Framework

Given that you're onboard with the concepts and principles in this book, here is a framework to plan your next three years of development, marketing, sales, and support.

Year 1: Plugin almost ready for beta testers

- Quarter 1
  - Start Twitter Account
  - Start Facebook Page (for later)
  - Build Landing Page for Beta Signups
  - Start Email Marketing Plan
- Quarter 2
  - Start email drip for Beta Signups
  - Collect their reviews

- If you plan on giving a discount on renewals, bump the price to allow for that

- Iterate; deploy

- Will you offer some lifetime licensing?

- Quarter 3

  - Launch Plugin

  - Tweet about your product availability

  - Show Your Plugin at a Meetup

  - Ask for reviews

- Quarter 4

  - Start your 18 month rolling budget; yearly licenses will renew in Q3 next year.

  - You should be at 500 followers/following on Twitter.

  - Is it time for outside support?

  - Consider a #CyberMonday Sale

Year 2: Plan for Profit

- Quarter 1

  - Review the last 3 quarters and get your 18 month rolling projection going.

  - Publish a blog post once a week.

  - Share on Twitter. You're building your own group of influencers (super fans).

  - Boost for $20 on your Facebook Page (1 per month).

- Quarter 2

  - Publish a blog post once a week.

  - Share on social.

  - Audit your marketing. Are you still sharing other people's posts? How about rewarding your super fans?

- Quarter 3

  - You should have about 1,000 followers on Twitter now.

- - Are you ready to outsource some marketing?

  - Are you ready to outsource or hire support?

  - How is your 18 month rolling budget going?

- Quarter 4

  - Ask for guest bloggers. ($150 a post budget)

  - Publish twice a month.

Year 3: Plan for Scale

- Quarter 1

  - Publish a Blog Post once a Week

  - Apply to Speak at one WordCamp or Meetup each quarter

  - Sponsor Your Local Meetup (Booth)

  - How's the budget tracking with reality?

  - Are you ready to hire another vendor or employee?

- Quarter 2

  - Sponsor a podcast

  - For the next iteration, audit your documentation.

- Quarter 3

  - Sponsor a Speaker or Two

  - Ask Users for What Features They Want

- Quarter 4

  - What's the next iteration? It's time to start again.

Add-on 2

Sample Marketing Brief

So if you go to this link, you can copy the sample document that follows into your own Google Drive. I have included more in the brief than you may want for the first campaign. Copy it and make a new one with your goals according to your plan on the three-year framework.

https://bit.ly/SampleMarketingBrief

H1: _____ Marketing Brief

[Insert your company name]

_____

[Insert your tagline here]

H2: Market Demographic

This [plugin shop] provides [product] for [customers] who [verb].

H2: Overall Goal

The primary goal is to increase plugin sales by 10% this year.

[Choose one goal. Stick to it. A download is a sale even if it is free.]

H2: Marketing Strategy

The primary strategy is to engage with current and potential white-label agencies in WordPress. This includes building relationships through commenting, social sharing, shared case studies, and minor website and social change.

H2: Product Branding

- Create a branding guideline even in a Google Doc. Don't worry about formatting for now. If the product has a coordinating brand to the company, that is best. Ensure you have this ready for when you hire social media managers, writers, and are ready to sponsor events.

- What is your font pairing?

- What are your primary, secondary, and tertiary colors in HEX codes?

- What kind of voice would you like the company to have? Kind, snarky, funny? Think of your audience. If you are selling something financial, stay serious.

H2: Website Content

Create a landing page for your product. Ensure that the product can be found from either your home page or a product menu in your main navigation.

Documentation might be controlled with versioning software and such. That's completely fine. Do what works best with your workflow. Don't be afraid to have a menu in the main navigation to your subdomain or other website url. Also, documentation is a treasure trove of gold for your marketing professional.

Make sure they have access to it and/or they know about it.

H2: Write a Product Tagline

A tagline can be funny, snarky, or reassuring. Pick something and stick with it. Try saying it out loud before you choose it.

H2: Write Case Studies (Use Cases)

Case studies are use cases that answer this question: "what problem does your product solve for me?"

- Case studies should be part of your "blog." It can be tagged as a case study for searchability or reorganization later.

- Case studies should include the client, the problem, the solution, and the results.

- Stick to that format - aim for 300 words.

- In the case study link to the client's website but be sure to have screenshots.

- Include before and after images where appropriate.

- Secure permission to share and/or include case study permission.

- Publish the case studies as you have them. (Strategically share on social.)

H2: Social Links

Be sure to include links to your social accounts on your company website. The product does not need it's own website and social handles. This duplicates work and dilutes your brand. You may want to save the usernames and have them direct to your company's main social accounts, however.

H2: Social Product Promotion

A phased approach will help the brand grow in a measured way. Growth in sales also includes growth in support. I've included the four primary B2B social networks in this marketing brief. If you were just starting, focus on Twitter.

[More detailed information on the mindset behind a successful social media presence is in my previous book Keys To Being Social, Being Real in a Virtual World. It is also available on Amazon.]

H3: Twitter

- I recommend setting up Twitter lists see https://bridgetwillard.com/twitterlists/

- Add #WordPress in your bio. Add your tagline in your bio.

- Follow everyone who follows you.

- Tweet once a day -- minimum.

- Share content from your peers and customers. Aim for 2 tweets sharing other people's content and one tweet for yourself.

- Spent ten minutes a day replying to people on Twitter.

H3: LinkedIn Company Page

- Post once a week something from your site.

- Post once a week something from a peer or white label partner. It would be good to create a list of your super fans and keep track of their content. You can curate this content from your Twitter lists.

- Always reply to comments as the brand.

- Ask employees to update their employment history to include the brand page. Stakeholders should do this as well.

H3: Facebook Page

- Post once a week something from your site.

- Post once a week something from another WordPress business or white label partner.

- Boost a post once a month with $20, defining the audience as WordPress agency. Be sure to include Instagram as a platform if you want to drive traffic.

- Reply to every comment as the Page.

- Comment on other Facebook Pages daily.

- (If you have a Facebook group, be present in the group daily.)

H3: Instagram

- Instagram is a good way to highlight your company culture for team building and recruiting.

- Tag people in the photos.. Who are you? Why do people want to be like you. The WP Buffs do a fantastic job at their company's Instagram.

- Use generic hashtags like #WordPress #RemoteWork and always TitleCase hashtags. You can use 6-12 hashtags per post.

- Spend time commenting on other Instagram accounts; not just liking.

- Ensure your Instagram account is a business account connected to your Facebook Page so you can boost posts. This way you can drive traffic to a landing page. Ideally, Instagram should be done with someone in house but it does take quite some time to build up a following.

This is the last place I would suggest spending resources.

Add-on 3

If You Don't Mind Your Business Who Will?

This is available as an ebook on my website but why not include it here, too?

You're busy. We get it. We're all busy.

Productivity Is About Choice

Don't hide behind productivity tools. We all have the same 24 hours a day. Working moms have children and extra responsibilities. Some work-at-home dads face the same. Single people have parents they care for or pets to take to the vet.

No matter what consumes your time, at some point, you have to control it. There is only so much a productivity app can do for you.

Your Business Must Be Your Priority

No matter how many assistants you hire, no one can care about your business more than you do. I learned this the hard way being a secretary for thirty years. As a content marketer since 2009, I have spoken to many business owners. Time constraints are an obstacle for us all.

The first step to working on your business is to stop accepting the lie. What lie? "I don't have time."

We all have time. We have a choice. We do the things that we value. So, if you don't work on your business who will?

Even if you hire a marketing agency, you still have to feed them content. You can't be found on the internet unless you're producing content. You need articles, landing pages on your website, videos, articles about your business, podcasts that feature your team members, etc.

Efficient Content Generation

Consistently coming up with content is about being efficient with your time and the information that crosses your physical or digital desk.

So? What are you going to do? Are you going to wait when you have time and things are slow? if they're slow that means you have no work.

Which means you haven't done the work ahead of time in order to fill up your production schedule. Marketing is a steam engine that needs to be constantly fed. You can coast for only so long before the lead generation train stops.

Just like any diet or fitness plan, you need two things: the plan and the work. Sometimes, it is the plan that becomes an overwhelming obstacle. So, here is your plan.

It's your responsibility to do the work.

Breakout each of the 50 business working weeks into topics. If you publish one piece of content every two weeks, you only need 25 in a year. If you publish one piece of content every four weeks, then you only need twelve a year.

The more you publish, the faster you will grow.

Map out your time. Map out your content. Do the work.

Map Out Your Time

This is a task that every business owner should do. I have dozens of content I have to produce for my clients every week. So, yeah.I get being busy. But my business matters, too.

What is my solution? Time blocking. I put in my Google Calendar "Blogging Time" as a recurring event every Friday from Noon to 2:00 PM. Then I make it a game. If I have time earlier in the week, and my video or article is produced, then I am free to do something else (fun) Friday afternoon. This is called psychological pairing. I reward myself for a job well done.

You can easily record a ten minute video and upload it to YouTube in an hour. You can also write an article that is 300-500 words. Make time for your business and treat it like it is a client meeting. You should be your own best client.

Map Out Your Content

The most effective marketing campaigns mean that your content should, as much as possible, be web first.

The point of marketing is to get people to your website, keep them reading, and cause them to do something (sign up, buy, etc.).

We call the "do something" a call to action.

Start a spreadsheet in Google Sheets with due dates. Fill it up with topics that come from your journal (see "What Should I Write About On My Blog?"). As you write these articles (or pieces of content), check off when they were finished and when they are published. Add a column for the link.

You will be amazed at how much content you can consistently produce and publish.

Do The Work

What Should I Write About On My Blog?

Keep a journal. It can be physical or it can be a document in Google Drive. But this journal should be dedicated to impactful moments in your business.

What's an impactful moment?

An impactful moment is something that makes you respond. This can be a positive event or a negative one. Both impact you. When is the last time a customer drove you nuts or made you proud? Write it down. What mistakes are your employees making? What do you wish you knew five years ago? Ten? Write it down.

These notes will be the topics of the articles and videos you publish. Social media posts serve to promote them.

Is My Website Ready for a Blog?

Yes. Presuming your website is on a content management system (CMS) like WordPress, you can easily blog (publish articles). If it isn't, Google "web developer" and go find one.

Ensure you have a Google Analytics account and that your website has that universal code. Your website should use Open Graph data and every page and article (post) should have a featured image (1200 x 628). If you don't know how to do this, find a web developer or reach out to me for a referral.

This will ensure that your content looks good when shared on social media. There are several image resources available to you including Unsplash.com and Canva.com. These are tools that are free.

Let go of the idea of perfection. Perfection is an unattainable goal. No one will ever reach it. This isn't print. It's the web. It can evolve and grow and change. You really only need 300-500 words. Most people can write this in a half hour once they know what they're writing. Voice to text is a great tool that most phones and Google Docs has it natively. I use it often.

Your business will never find its voice unless you start.

Start with the journal.

Using Different Types of Content in Marketing

Various types of content is the key to ensuring your business has the answers your audience (and potential customers) are looking for.

You could start with a marketing persona. However, I find that most small business owners see this as an obstacle. Forget out the persona. Who buys your products? Who do you serve? Don't think of an imaginary person; think of an actual customer.

Writing for your company website is meant to serve your customers, not you. Keep that in the front of your mind. As the business owner, you are well-equipped to write these articles. If you need an editor, find one. They are easy to find. I'll be happy to refer you to several.

Draw inspiration from your journal and start typing. Hire an editor if you must. Otherwise, edit 24 hours after you have written the piece.

Below are eight different types of content. If you published two of each kind, you'd have sixteen pieces of content for the year. That's four more than the twelve you need to publish once a month. Granted, most of your content should be articles or videos. That said, a mixture isn't a bad thing.

Articles

Articles appear on your blog and can (potentially) be found in a search. Voice search with Alexa and Siri are increasing. Keep the tone of your articles friendly and conversational. Use humor if it matches your personality or the personality you want your company to have (we call this brand voice).

HemingwayApp.com is a great resource for grammar as well as Grammarly.com. I would also highly recommend purchasing "Everybody Writes" by Ann Handley.

I personally write in Google Docs. It's free. There's really no reason why you shouldn't also use this tool. It makes collaboration easy, especially if you don't physically publish the article on your website.

Video

Video is one of the easiest forms of content to produce. We all have video cameras in our hands. Most of us sit at computers that also allow us to record.

Record your video, upload it to YouTube, add a description and title, and publish. It's that easy.

Now, you can embed that video in a blog post on your website and publish it as an article with a short description.

If you want to do more, use Headliner.app to add music and captions. You can also take advantage of Facebook and Instagram Live as well as Instagram's IGTV.

Landing Pages

Landing pages are pages on your website with one focus and call to action (CTA) in mind. It should be as distraction-free as possible. The copy should get to the point as quickly as possible. Don't talk about yourself. Talk about how this product or service solves your customer's problem. Focus on one thing. Only one thing.

Articles About Your Business

People want to know more about you and your company. Your website's About Page should be more than one photo and a 50-word blurb. Why did you start your business? Who is the founder? Where were you on important dates in history? What inspires you? How do you use your free time?

This humanizes your brand and allows customers to connect with you. Connection leads to loyalty. Loyalty leads to sales.

Podcast Interviews

So many podcasts need guests. Generally, that is how podcast hosts generate their content. If there is a podcast in your area of expertise, reach out to the host. Send them a note through their website or email that is kind and friendly. Don't have your secretary do this. This is one thing that annoys us as podcast hosts. (We get that a lot.)

Then give the podcast host a short reason (100 words) why you should be on their show. Be politie. Kindness makes a huge difference.

Case Studies

Don't be afraid of case studies. They don't need to be 2,000 word white papers. In fact, unless it's for a medical journal, they shouldn't be.

Instead, create a standard questionnaire with five to seven questions. Email your customer and ask her if she'd like to participate. What was the problem? What was the solution? What are the results?

These answers can be used as is or a study can be written from them. Case studies are a step up from customer reviews and are powerful lead generators.

Customer Interviews

Go beyond a case study by interviewing your customers. The most loyal ones will love to participate. Where did they use your product, how, and what is their favorite place to use it? Have fun with the questions. Ask for photos of them using the product. Incentivize this with discounts or $25 Amazon Gift Cards. It works well.

Customer Reviews

It's so hard to ask for reviews. But your past and current customers won't know you need them unless you ask. Find a place in your company's workflow to ask for them in a nice, polite way -- at the right time. Only you know when the right time to ask is.

Yearly Content Map

This section will help you map out your content throughout the year, drawing inspiration from your journal and the above-stated content types.

Start with an achievable goal: One Published Piece of Content Each Month

January

Topic Theme: Topics for the beginning of the year could include starting new habits, using your products in a good way, or even a discount for your services to start the new year right.

This is less-than evergreen but easily achievable.

Topic Type: Aim for an article.

February

Topic Theme: The year is going well and an easy theme is love. Show love to your customers by interviewing a loyal customer. This can be done with video and transcribed and/or through a questionnaire over email.

Topic Type: Aim for a customer interview.

March

Topic Theme: With March comes spring and our fondness for the outdoors, cleaning, and even luck. Though some of these topics are more closely related to a holiday than others, those types of themes help spring up memories. Why did you start this business? Why is this your passion?

Topic Type: Aim for an article about your business.

April

Topic Theme: Fools ask foolish questions and do foolish things. Everyone has things they wish their customers knew about their products or services before they purchase. Mistakes are a great way to inform and entertain future customers. Be sure to keep it generic, though. You want to avoid shaming the customer.

Topic Type: Aim for an article that educates.

May

Topic Theme: Summer is around the corner and if your business is seasonal, you may have a bit of extra time or be swamped. It generally depends on your business. Go to your inspiration journal and look for a case study that can be written. Get the content published before people start going on vacations.

Topic Type: Aim for a case study.

June

Topic Theme: Patriotic holidays, vacations, and school being out are popular themes during this time of year. Less seasonal, however, would be a video showing or demonstrating the use of your product or service. Make sure it is less than ten minutes long. It can be uploaded to YouTube, Facebook, LinkedIn, and even IGTV.

Topic Type: Aim for a video.

July

Topic Theme: Freedom, cookouts, and sweltering weather are popular topics for the northern hemisphere. If you're south of the equator, you're in winter. Both of those extremes lead to great types of content to create. So many podcast hosts need guests during the "dead of winter" and "heat of summer." They may have even had cancelations. You can post a recap of this podcast on your website as a blog post (100 words) with a link to where people can listen.

Topic Type: Aim to be a podcast guest.

August

Topic Theme: What is one thing you wish your customers knew about your industry? Write about that. We all have those pain points where people think our jobs are easier than they are. Show your value by educating your audience about the certifications or hurdles you had to overcome to have your career.

Topic Type: Aim for an informative article.

September

Topic Theme: September historically marks the end of the harvest and time to go back to school. Your business can create a video on how to use one of your products to make their lives a bit easier. Think of how your service or product can be used in a larger context.

Context answers the "why" of your products and services. Make sure the video is less than ten minutes long. It can be uploaded to YouTube, Facebook, LinkedIn, and even IGTV.

Topic Type: Aim for video that educates with context.

October

Topic Theme: Fall in the Northern Hemisphere and Spring in the Southern Hemisphere are times of death and renewal. This is an excellent time to write an article about productivity and inspiration.

Topic Type: Aim for an inspirational article.

November

Topic Theme: November is typically a time to be thankful. This is a great time of year to ask for customer reviews and publish them throughout your website as appropriate. If you have an eCommerce store, product reviews are best placed on that product page. Showing your gratitude for customers who give your reviews can be done with $5 coffee shop cards or discounts on future orders.

Topic Type: Aim for customer reviews.

December

Topic Theme: The end of the year is a time of nostalgia for most cultures regardless of which holidays are celebrated. This is an excellent time to write about the origins of your business or something you're especially thankful for in your industry.

Topic Type: Aim for an article about your business.

Business Affirmation

My business is important to me. I deserve to dedicate time each week to build my business both in person and on the web. I am an expert in my field. I help my customers and clients. I enjoy helping others.

I promise myself to block time in my calendar to work on my own marketing. I am dedicating this year to spend this time and watch my business grow. More importantly, I will allow myself to grow, find my voice, and be heard in my industry.

Journal Prompts

1. Why did you start your business? How has your career lead you to this point?

2. List five things you wish your clients knew about your industry. How can you help them learn more?

3. Track your time for one day. What surprised you the most? How many hours did you spend working on your business instead of in it?

4. What distracted you the most today? How could you help prevent that from happening?

5. When was the last time you felt discouraged? What cheered you up and how can that help transform how you do business?

6. What type of customers do you empathize with the most? Why do you think that?

7. How much does it cost your business to have you working? Meaning, how much do you cost per hour? What tasks did you do

today that were well below your pay grade?

8. What keeps you from delegating tasks? How do you think you could train someone?

9. What is one thing in your business you wish you didn't have to do? How can you outsource or hire for that work?

10. When is the last time you documented the systems and processes in your business? What happens to your business if something happens to you?

11. When is the last time regret helped you prevent a poor business decision?

12. Where would you like to be next year? How can you break that goal into actionable steps?

BIBLIOGRAPHY

American Marketing Association. "Definitions
of Marketing." AMA,.org,
https://www.ama.org/the-definition-of-
marketing-what-is-marketing/. Accessed
15 Feb 2021.

Annex Cloud, and Sean Ogino. "Overcoming The
Discount Addiction With Loyalty."
https://www.annexcloud.com/, Annex
Cloud,
https://www.annexcloud.com/blog/overc
oming-discount-addiction-loyalty/.
Accessed 30 Dec 2020.

Beaver Builder. "Affiliate Agreement."
WPBeaverBuilder.com, 1 Apr 2019,
https://www.wpbeaverbuilder.com/affilia
te-program-terms-conditions/.

Business Insider, and AJ Caldwell. "Why top
automakers spend millions on concept
cars they don't plan on making." Business
Insider, 23 Apr 2019,
https://www.businessinsider.com/automa

kers-spend-millions-on-concept-cars-t hey-dont-make-2019-4.

CX Optimization Agency. "Product Lifecycle Marketing: What Matters Most at Every Stage." cxl.com, 25 Sep 2020, https://cxl.com/blog/product-lifecycle-m arketing/.

Denning, Alex. "Marketing channels, and how to think about marketing your WordPress business." getellipsis.com, https://getellipsis.com/blog/marketing-c hannels-for-wordpress/. Accessed 9 Dec 2020.

Freemius, and Vova Feldman. "How to Outrank Your Competitors' SEO on The NEW WordPress.org Plugin Repository." Freemius.com, 29 Sept 2020, https://freemius.com/blog/seo-on-new-plugin-repository/.

Freemius, and Vova Feldman. "Lifetime license for WordPress plugins – the right way!" Freemius.com, https://freemius.com/blog/lifetime-licen

se-for-wordpress-plugins-the-right-wa
y/. Accessed 31 Dec 2020.

Freemius, and Vito Peleg. "How to Have a
$100k+ WordPress Product Launch."
Freemius.com, 1 Apr 2020,
https://freemius.com/blog/100k-wordpre
ss-product-launch/.

Frog-Dog.com. "How Much Should Companies
Budget for Marketing?"
https://www.frog-dog.com/,
https://www.frog-dog.com/magazine/ho
w-much-should-companies-budget-for-
marketing. Accessed 18 Dec 2020.

Guru99. "Alpha Testing Vs Beta Testing: What's
the Difference?" Guru99.com,
https://www.guru99.com/alpha-beta-tes
ting-demystified.html. Accessed 15 Feb
2021.

Hall, Amy. "Drip Campaigns and Nurture
Campaigns." AmyHall.biz,
https://amyhall.biz/blog/2019/04/03/drip
-campaigns-nurture-campaigns/.
Accessed 30 Dec 2020.

Indie Hackers. "Leaving My Equity Trading Career to Build a WordPress Business." indiehackers.com, https://www.indiehackers.com/interview/leaving-my-equity-trading-career-to-build-a-wordpress-business-cd10ed8057. Accessed 31 Dec 2020.

Laine-Naida, Warren. "Learn About HTML In 5 Steps." Warren Laine-Naida // Digital Consulting, https://warrenlainenaida.net/2020-11-learn-about-html-in-5-steps/. Accessed 17 November 2020.

Make WordPress. "Plugin Unit Tests." WordPress.org, https://make.wordpress.org/cli/handbook/misc/plugin-unit-tests/. Accessed 7 Dec 2020.

Pagely.com, and Joshua Strebel. "Blue Oceans. Notes on Joshua Strebel's WCPHX Keynote presentation (Part 2)." Pagely.com, https://pagely.com/blog/wcphx-keynote-2/. Accessed 31 Dec 2020.

Post Status, and Brian Krogsgard. "The
    WordPress product market is completely
    different now." PostStatus.com, 30 Oct
    2017,
    https://poststatus.com/wordpress-produ
    ct-market-completely-different-now/#c
    omment-323304.

SaaSquatch. "The Psychology Behind Loyalty
    Programs." SaaSquatch.com,
    https://www.saasquatch.com/blog/psycho
    logy-behind-loyalty-programs/.
    Accessed 30 Dec 20.

Sivers, Derek. "Obvious to you. Amazing to
    others." YouTube, YouTube, 28 Jun 2011,
    https://youtu.be/xcmI5SSQLmE. Accessed
    3 Dec 2020.

Vasquez, Ales J. "WordPress Community: Giving
    Back at a Nonprofit Hackathon - WPblab."
    WPwatercooler Network, 13 Oct 2016,
    https://www.wpwatercooler.com/smartm
    arketingshow/wpblab-048-wordpress-co
    mmunity-giving-back-at-a-nonprofit-h
    ackathon-wpblab/. Accessed 29 Dec 2020.

WordPress.tv, and Devin Walker. "Using Third
    Party Code to Create Unique and
    Meaningful Solutions." WordPress.tv, 28
    Apr 2016,
    https://wordpress.tv/2016/04/28/devin-
    walker-using-third-party-code-to-creat
    e-unique-and-meaningful-solutions/.

WPRocket. "3 Reasons Why You Shouldn't Offer
    Lifetime Licences – Transparency Report
    8 (August/September 2015)."
    wp-rocket.me,
    https://wp-rocket.me/blog/3-reasons-w
    hy-you-shouldnt-offer-lifetime-licences
    -transparency-report-8-augustseptembe
    r-2015/. Accessed 31 Dec 2020.

WP Starters, and Leo Koo. "5 Reasons Lifetime
    WordPress Licenses Are Bad For You."
    WPStarters.com, 26 Jul 2016,
    https://www.wpstarters.com/faqs/dont-b
    uy-lifetime-wordpress-licenses/.

WPwatercooler, and Rhonda Negard. "EP180 –
    How to Show Your Personality Through
    Your Brand." WPwatercooler Network,
WPwatercooler Network, 18 Dec 2020,
    https://www.wpwatercooler.com/smartm

arketingshow/ep180-how-to-show-your -personality-through-your-brand/.

WPwatercooler Network. "Funding Open Source With Agency Work — How Plugins Are Really Built." WPwatercooler Network, 31 Jan 2020, https://www.wpwatercooler.com/wpblab/ wpblab-ep145-funding-open-source-wit h-agency-work-how-plugins-are-really -built/. Accessed 12 Dec 202.

WPwatercooler Network. "Pros and Cons of Business Models in Open Source." WPwatercooler Network, 6 Mar 2020, https://www.wpwatercooler.com/wpblab/ wpblab-ep149-pros-and-cons-of-busine ss-models-in-open-source/. Accessed 12 Dec 2020.

Final Thank You!

Hey thanks for reading this book. If you liked it, feel free to give it a five star rating on Amazon.com. Don't forget to tweet it out and tell your friends.

Thanks again,

Your friend,

Bridget